PSALMS
Songs of Discipleship

PSALMS

Songs of Discipleship

Volume 3

PSALMS 101-150

by

ROBERT ALDEN

MOODY PRESS

CHICAGO

INTRODUCTION

This is the third and concluding volume of observations on the Hebrew Psalter. I trust that these remarks will deepen the appreciation of Scripture and of this portion of the Psalms in particular.

Though there are many unanswered questions in the Psalms—questions of language, custom, theology—it is hard to miss the main lessons. The Psalms, like all other Scripture, are for our teaching, rebuke, correction, and training in righteousness, so that we may be thoroughly equipped for every good work (see 2 Ti 3:16-17).

Many of the remarks are of a technical nature, but many are of a devotional nature too. Scholarship ought not be divorced from piety. Obviously, not every word or even every verse can receive comment in an endeavor of this scope, but perhaps what is included will whet the appetite for even more concentrated Bible study.

As in the first one hundred psalms, these last fifty evidence great variety. We find here psalms that expose the innermost feelings of God's ancient people. Some of the psalms may lead to tears; others should evoke profound joy. Different psalms are for different moods. If you know what the themes of the psalms are, you can select one to meet your spiritual need: "Rejoice with them that do rejoice and weep with them that weep" (Ro 12:15).

This group of psalms has an above-average number of public or liturgical works. So think of standing before the tabernacle in the days of David or in the Temple precincts in later years. Imagine worshiping with believers of a bygone era. Put yourself in the ensemble or in the chorus as it lifted its praise to God who lived then, who is alive today, and who will live forevermore. In other words, enter into the sweet spirit of praise, join the anthem of exaltation, and let the hymnbook of ancient Israel become part of your spontaneous worship of God your Saviour.

PSALM 101

Psalm 101 may fall into the category of wisdom psalms or royal psalms. Many of its sentiments reflect the teaching of Proverbs. Compare verse 4 with Proverbs 11:20, verse 5*b* with Proverbs 6:17, and verse 7 with Proverbs 25:5.

The title states that it is a psalm of David. If one reads the eight verses of the psalm with a king in mind, it sounds like a code of royal ethical behavior. The psalm takes the form of a protestation of integrity, justice, and piety. The things the king is *for,* as well as the things he is *against,* receive equal emphasis. He is for wisdom, perfection, and faith; and he is against baseness, perversity, evil, slander, pride, and deceit. Every verse and every stich within each verse, except for the last, contain the pronouns *I, me,* or *my.*

The opening two verses strike a positive note in general terms, with the twin virtues of covenant faithfulness (Heb. *hesed*) and justice as the first words in the Hebrew text.

The only problem in the psalm is the explanation of the question in the middle of verse 2: "When will you come to me?" (J.B.). If the reading and translation are correct, it may be a rhetorical way of expressing the wish, "Please, Lord, be with me."

The poem continues in verses 3-5 with claims of innocence. David resists any identification with evil deeds or

7

wicked people. Not only is he pure, but he does not look with approval on sin (v. 3*a*), and he hates those who commit such things (v. 3*b*). The word "know" in verse 4, as in other places it occurs, has a very broad meaning. It includes cognizance, experience, intimate participation, and even love.

Verse 6 turns once more to the positive side of things. Whereas in verse 3 David would not set his eyes on anything base, in verse 6 he says he would set them on the faithful people of the land. From the end of verse 6 through verse 7 the psalm reads like the hiring policy at David's palace. Those who serve must walk in a perfect way, must not be deceitful or tell lies. In a broader sense, the entire nation was the household of the king. Perhaps this policy is a general outline of the judicial system in ancient Israel. This last observation is supported by verse 8, which expands the coverage of this justice to include the city of the LORD, Jerusalem, and the land, Israel. The expression "morning by morning" (ASV) points to the regular meeting sessions of the court.

The modern believer, of course, is not on David's throne, but he is responsible for applying these standards to his own life. Verse 3 warns us to keep only pure scenes before our eyes. Verse 5 states the fact that talking evil behind a neighbor's back is abhorrent to God. Verse 7 demands that we be absolutely honest. Verse 8 reminds us to examine our lives daily for sins and to destroy them before they destroy us.

Only as we meet these requirements and seek to conform our lives to the tenets of Psalm 101 can we sing of God's loving-kindness and justice, and behave wisely in a perfect way (vv. 1-2).

PSALM 102

Psalm 102 divides easily into three parts: verses 1-11 record the believer's complaint, verses 12-22 contain praise to God for His mercy to Zion, and verses 23-28 meditate on the brevity of human life and the eternality of God.

The opening third of this psalm describes in as desperate terms as may be found anywhere the plight of the man who feels cursed by God. Affliction is not seen as punishment for sin or as chastening for righteousness' sake but, rather, is without a reason. Although the afflicted appeals to God's mercy, there is no hint of repentance.

After the initial two verses, which are a prayer for mercy, there follows a catalog of unpleasantries. In highly poetic style the author of this psalm describes his lack of appetite (v. 4), the quick passage of his brief years (vv. 3, 11), his malnutrition (v. 5), his loneliness (vv. 6-7), his abuse by enemies (v. 8), and his sadness (v. 9). The imagery is quite rich. Note for instance brevity of life compared to smoke (v. 3) and grass (v. 11); solitude compared to the habits of the pelican, owl, and sparrow (vv. 6-7); and food and drink compared to ashes and tears (v. 9).

The first and third sections of this psalm go well together with the focus on fast-approaching death. Compare verses 3 and 11 with verses 23 and 24. The middle section fits with the last section by emphasizing God's eternality. Notice verse 12 and verses 25-27.

Verses 12-22 are not so much a prayer for deliverance of Zion as an anticipation of that deliverance. This ancient poet is sure that just as God is eternal and sovereign so will He see to the preservation of His holy city. These verses are the only clue to the date of the work. Apparently Jerusalem is under siege, already destroyed, or its people are exiled.

The expression at the end of verse 13 is similar to Isaiah 61:2 (MLB), "The year of the LORD's favor." In due time, when He has all circumstances ready and at the most propitious moment, God will act. That time had arrived, according to verse 13, and so God's restoration of Zion will have the greatest apologetic value. Unbelieving nations and foreign powers will have to notice that there is a God who acts on behalf of His people. Those who have been destitute can use these blessed facts for their own encouragement, for the persuasion of outsiders, and for strengthening that heritage of faith for their descendants. The psalm builds almost to eschatological proportions at verse 22, where we see people of all races and languages, realms and ages, gathered to serve the King of kings.

The third part of the psalm, verses 23-28, is familiar because Hebrews 1:10-12 is a quotation of verses 25-27. Both here and in Hebrews the everlasting nature of the godhead is in view. Naturally, with the limited revelation available in Old Testament times, one thinks of God the Father in these verses, but the author of Hebrews ascribes them to God the Son, the Lord Jesus Christ. He participated in the creation (v. 25), He lives forever (v. 27), and He is unchangeable (v. 26). Together with John 1:3, verse 25 is one of the best for showing that Christ was active at the genesis of the world.

This whole third section is spoken by a man aware of approaching death, but full of assurance in the everlasting God. Though his days are short and his strength failing, he knows God who is the opposite of all human frailty. Though we are like old garments and withering grass, our God is the Creator, the Sustainer, and the immutable Lord of heaven and earth.

10

PSALM 103

"Bless the LORD, O my soul" both begins and ends this well-known psalm. Other verses within it are familiar and beloved also. Verse 10 reads:

> He hath not dealt with us after our sins;
> nor rewarded us according to our iniquities.

And verse 13:

> Like as a father pitieth his children,
> so the LORD pitieth them that fear him.

Some people are confused by the word "bless." God blesses us and we are told to bless God. "How can we be God's benefactor?" they rightly ask. The answer is to be found in the broader meaning of the Hebrew word which lies behind the translation. It is correctly rendered by the word "bless," but it means both to get good things from God and to give good things back to God. One of the few things we are in any position to return to God is praise; hence in this psalm and elsewhere "bless" means "praise."

Even more interesting is the root from which the Hebrew word comes. The same root letters are in the noun "knee" and hence the related verb is "kneel." Ancient blessings between fathers and sons and between sovereigns and subjects were made with the latter kneeling at the knee of the former. Hence "to bless" may mean "to kneel" as well as "to bestow divine gifts."

This psalm does have evidence of plan in it. Not only the same words of injunction both open and close the psalm but there is a loose chiastic structure. Note the following proposed outline:

The first section is composed of the admonition to praise the Lord *who* does such and such. There are five relative clauses which describe all the things God did and does, things which we ought not to forget. He forgives all our sin. This is our first and most desperate need in terms of His demands and our inability. He heals all our diseases. If we might spiritualize here, He cures us of the fatal cancer of sin. He redeems us from destruction. He saves us forever. He repossesses us from His enemy and the enemy of our souls. He crowns us with loving-kindness and tender mercy. Then He satisfies our desires with good things. By this time our desires are His desires and He delights so to bless us. Without these daily provisions our lives would be impossible.

The section on God's being and doings is an abbreviated list of God's attributes in poetic form. Verse 6 speaks of His justice, verse 8 of His mercy, verse 11 of His love, and verse 14 of His omniscience. In addition, verse 7 speaks of His revelation to Moses and the people of Israel.

This is a blessed psalm not only because of the admonition to "bless the LORD" at its beginning and end, but also because there is almost nothing of God's anger or punishment in it. It is for God's redeemed people, and its truths neither apply to the unregenerate nor may be appropriated by them. The second section on God's doings makes this distinction. Verse 17 indicates that His loving-kindness, His covenant love, is for those who fear and reverence Him. Man, though finite and temporal, may have a blessed, everlasting heritage through membership in God's family, "to such as keep his covenant, and to those that remember his commandments to do them" (v. 18).

The closing section exhorts the whole creation, heaven and earth, to praise God. His mighty angels, who have the privilege of seeing Him firsthand as well as we, the works of His hands, are enjoined to bless Him. Verses 20 and 21 are probably addressed to those heavenly creatures under the terms "angels," "hosts," and "ministers." Each reader, however, is under the same orders when he reads the last words of this blessed psalm: "Bless the LORD, O my soul."

PSALM 104

Psalm 104, like Psalm 103, begins and ends with the words, "Bless the LORD, O my soul." The outline of Psalm 104, however, is not as discernible as the one in the psalm which precedes it. These thirty-five verses constitute a majestic hymn of praise to God, especially for His creative and sustaining power.

In a very general way, the psalm follows the order of creation in Genesis. The light of Genesis 1:3 appears in verse 2. The cover of water and the subsequent appearance of the dry land (Gen 1:2, 9) correspond to verses 6 and 7. The growth of the herbs and grass (Gen 1:11-12) appears in verse 14, and the daily and monthly divisions of Genesis 1: 14-18 receive mention in verse 20.

The New American Bible offers this broad outline for Psalm 104:

The marvels of atmosphere and sky (vv. 1-4)
   of the dry land and ocean (vv. 5-9)

13

of the streams and fields that give drink and food to
man, beast, and bird (vv. 10-18)

of the sun and moon with the activities of day and
night (vv. 19-23)

of the manifold life in the mighty sea (vv. 24-26)

The Lord governs and sustains all His creatures (vv. 27-
30)

God's omnipotence and sanctity (vv. 31-35)

The language is very lofty and picturesque throughout.
From the beginning this psalm illustrates the Hebrew pen-
chant for describing concepts and relationships in concrete
terms. Note in verse 1 how God is clothed with honor and
majesty. In verse 2 He is dressed in light. According to verse
3, He rides on the clouds and walks on the wind.

Verse 4 is quoted in Hebrews 1:7, where the writer is
arguing for the superiority of Christ over angels. "Angel"
and "messenger" are alternate translations of the same Hebrew and Greek words. In Psalm 104 they are wind and fire,
which serve God. In Hebrews, Christ is over them in the
ranks of superhuman beings.

Job 38:9-11 somewhat parallels verses 5-7, especially as
the waters are viewed as a garment for the earth and as God
has set boundaries for the oceans.

From the cosmic descriptions of God's creative activity
(vv. 1-9), the psalmist begins at verse 10 to examine the
more mundane and everyday features of His providence.
Not only is God responsible for seas, winds, and clouds, but
He also provides food and drink for all animal life. A certain orderliness characterizes the earth, with all its natural
processes moving like clockwork to the benefit of all. So
trees are for birds (v. 17), mountains are for goats (v. 18),

14

and all are to enjoy the grass and herbs (v. 14) watered by rivers and springs (v. 10), which ultimately get their water from the sky, God's chambers (v. 13).

Verse 15 is a beautiful and well-known reference to the three basic crops of the ancient Palestinian: grapes, olives, and grain. These supplied his three basic commodities: wine, oil, and bread (cf. Deu 24:19-21). Oil had several uses: for cooking, to make perfumed lotions, to combat skin dryness, as medicine, and to fuel lamps.

Just as in verses 18 and 19 certain animals lived in certain places, so in verses 20-22 different animals have special times to hunt and hide. Man too fits into this elaborate scheme by being a daytime worker (v. 23).

Verse 24 is a kind of doxology inserted at a point where the psalmist seems overwhelmed by the intricacies and magnificence of God's wise operations.

After two verses relating to activities in and on the seas, God's provision of food for all is once more emphasized (vv. 27-28). Just as God is in control of life, so death comes to all creatures (v. 29). This too is part of His sovereign design for the world.

The concluding five verses of the psalm read like a prayer with several jussives ("let" forms expressing mild commands). The worshiper wishes himself to be constantly and everlastingly praising God. As in Psalm 19:14, he prays that his thoughts, as well, might be sweet and hence acceptable to God (v. 34).

Only verse 35 has a negative note, although the ancient servant of God probably would not agree. God is glorified, he would protest, both by blessing the righteous and by cursing the wicked. Not to punish the sinner would be unjust. So, coupled with all the lovely thoughts of verses 31-35 is

the imprecation against the enemies of God. But even in this
the poet enjoins his soul once more to bless the Lord.

PSALM 105

Psalm 105 is like Psalm 78 in that they both recite the
history of Israel. As Psalm 104 speaks of the history and
operation of the creation, so Psalm 105 praises God for His
faithfulness to the Abrahamic covenant in giving the Israelites the promised land. The story goes from the father of
the faithful to the occupation of Canaan.

For purposes of study, the psalm's forty-five verses divide
into several pericopes. Verses 1-6 are a general invitation
to praise, indicating that perhaps this composition was for
some festival. God's faithful keeping of the Abrahamic covenant is the theme of verses 7-11. Verses 12-15 briefly speak
of the wanderings of the patriarchs. Then the life of Joseph
is summarized (vv. 16-22). The next three verses capsulize
the 400 years in Egypt. Verses 26-36 speak of Moses and
the Egyptian plagues. Then the Exodus and the forty years
of wanderings come into view (vv. 37-42). The final three
verses summarize the whole poem and end on a note of praise
to God for bringing His people into the promised land.

If the "praise the LORD" (Heb., *hallelujah*) at the end of
Psalm 104 goes at the beginning of Psalm 105, as the Vul-
gate translation of the Old Testament indicates, then this
psalm both begins and ends with the same words. (It would
also make the opening and closing words of Psalm 104 match
more perfectly.)

In 1 Chronicles 16:8-22 are found the first fifteen verses

16

of Psalm 105. Other comparisons exist between verse 36 and Psalm 78:51; verse 39 and 78:14; and verse 40 and 78:24.

A series of imperatives opens the psalm. Note the injunctions to give thanks, call, make known, sing, praise, talk, glory, rejoice, seek, and remember (vv. 1-5). This psalm especially emphasizes a note of remembrance. We are to remember (v. 5) that God has not forgotten His covenant (v. 8). As the historical section begins with that idea, so it ends the same way. Verse 42 states once more that He remembered His holy word and Abraham His servant.

The essence of the promise is in verse 11: "Unto thee will I give the land of Canaan." Then the body of the psalm traces the events from Abraham, who first received that promise, to its fulfillment under Joshua (v. 44). The only major events left out are those connected with Mount Sinai and the giving of the Law. However, Moses and the Law do receive passing mention in verses 26 and 45.

As is the case elsewhere, even in the New Testament, the picture is drawn to show the people as weak and God as strong. So in verses 12-17, the people of Abraham are few and homeless. They are moved by hunger only to prove that it is God who sustains and protects them.

It is interesting that the patriarchs are called "anointed" ones and "prophets" in verse 15. Although they wrote no Bible books, they were, in their time, the chosen spokesmen for the living God.

Joseph receives unusual emphasis with details added, such as the chains of verse 18, which are not mentioned in the Genesis account. Again, note how the strength of God is made perfect through the weakness of man; in fact, God's righteousness overrules the wickedness of men.

The psalmist is committed to the sovereignty of God, as verse 25 indicates. It was not that the Egyptians merely

17

turned against the Israelites, but God was responsible for this hatred toward His people. But remember the larger picture: God wanted to fulfill His promise and that could not be done as long as they were welcome and prosperous in Egypt.

The plagues listed in verses 28-36 are not in the same order as in the book of Exodus (chaps. 7-12). In fact, the murrain (Ex 9:3) and boils (Ex 9:9) are not mentioned in Psalm 105, but rather the breaking down of vines and trees (v. 33), which is excluded from the Exodus account.

The many events of the wanderings are passed over quickly with only the pillars of fire and cloud (Ex 13:21-22), quails (Ex 16:13), manna (Ex 16:14-16), and water from the rock (Ex 17:1-7) receiving mention. These, of course, are the great positive things God did for them. The next psalm, 106, gives much more emphasis to the bad behavior of the Israelites, but this psalm underscores instead the fidelity of God.

An almost humorous note penetrates at verse 38 where the psalmist records that Egypt was glad to see Israel leave.

The summary verses consummate the account and also give, as it were, a moral to the story. The deliverance itself, as well as the recounting of it, has a purpose. That purpose is to make God's people keep His statutes and laws. The whole duty of man is to obey and praise the Lord.

PSALM 106

With Psalm 106 the fourth book within the Psalter comes to a close. Verse 48 of the psalm is a kind of doxology or benediction very similar to the phrases that end the other divisions (cf. Ps 41:13, 72:18-19, 89:52, and 150:6). Also note that a hallelujah opens and closes the psalm.

Praise, prayer, and confession are the categories into which this, another historical psalm, falls. By far the majority of verses recount the ingratitude, infidelity, and undependability of the Israelite forefathers. So, while the psalm coincides with the preceding ones, being replete with scriptural allusions and historical illustrations, the emphasis is on the depravity of God's people rather than on His covenant faithfulness.

The opening verse is the same as 1 Chronicles 16:34 and Psalm 107:1 and 136:1, and is similar to many other verses sprinkled throughout the Psalms. It introduces the first five verses which, with the last two, are the only ones outside the review of the calamitous disobediences of the ancient Hebrews.

Although verse 6 has the pronoun "we," the rest of the psalm talks about "them"—the fathers who left Egypt, rebelled all through the desert wanderings, and eventually reaped their harvest of faithlessness in the exile (v. 46).

The account begins with the actual Exodus from Egypt. And, just as Exodus 14:11-12 records, the people were rebellious even on the Egyptian shore of the Red Sea. At that early point they began questioning Moses directly and God indirectly. But God took away their doubts by the mighty miracle of the dried-up sea, which at the same time destroyed the enemy. Only after that did the redeemed believe God and praise Him (Ex 15:1-21).

This order of events points up the basic carnality and infidelity of the people. They were the kind who would not believe unless they could see. They were the sort who could be convinced only by the most extravagant and obvious of miracles. They walked by sight and not by faith.

The episode alluded to in verses 13-15 is most likely the incident at the waters of Marah, which follows immediately after the songs of Moses and Miriam in Exodus 15. Again, note how quickly the Israelites forgot God's deliverance and started thinking of their own problems. As a result of their bitter complaint God "gave them their request; but sent leanness into their soul." This is a frightening indictment on these children of God who thought mainly of their comfort and never saw themselves as actors in God's drama of redemption. This is a very easy verse to apply to modern Western Christianity because in every community of believers there are satisfied bodies hosting starving souls; wealthy purses and impoverished hearts.

The events of Numbers 16 are the background of verses 16-18. Korah, Dathan, and Abiram arrogantly challenged the authority of Moses and Aaron and paid for their insolence with their lives.

But while in verse 16 Aaron is called a saint or holy one (a person "set apart" by and for God), referring to his office as high priest, he was the one mainly responsible for the golden calf, the next episode cited in Psalm 106 (vv. 19-23). Exodus 32 records the tragic turn of events which led the nation to the very brink of extinction. Only the intercession of Moses moved God to spare them.

When the twelve spies were sent to investigate Canaan (Num 13), the people accepted the majority's pessimistic report and chose not to obey God and attack (Num 14). That is the backdrop of verse 24.

Baal-peor (v. 28) was a Moabite deity which attracted worship from the Israelites, according to Numbers 25:3. Naturally, this syncretism angered the Lord and He was about to annihilate them when Phinehas, Aaron's grandson, intervened after 24,000 had died from the divinely sent plague.

Again the people angered God, this time at Meribah (vv. 32-33). Numbers 20:2-13 provides the details of this unfortunate act of unbelief on the part of the Israelites. The last example of little faith and disregard of God's will the psalmist chose is from Judges 1. Over and over in that chapter, one reads that this or that tribe did not drive out the inhabitants of the areas they were to possess. In addition, they intermarried and they adulterated their worship of Yahweh with idolatry. They even adopted the abominable practices of the heathen, such as child sacrifice (v. 38), which were outright transgressions of God's written Law. All this compounded the anger of God against them until ultimately He judged them with the Babylonian captivity (vv. 41-43).

Yet even in that most dreadful of punishments God was faithful to His covenant. According to verses 44 and 45, He heard their cry and reversed Himself, as His great mercy would demand.

Against this bleak background, the patient and enduring love of God shines clearly and brightly. And to that love the psalmist appeals when he prays in verse 47 (NASB), "Save us, O LORD our God, and gather us from among the nations."

God's people were little different in Babylon than they were in Egypt. And they are little different now than they were 3,000 years ago. They still question God at other Meribahs; they substitute new Baals; they fail to muster for His marching orders. But though we are like ancient Israel, God is as gracious and full of pity now as He was then. His ear is still open to the penitent's cry, and His hand is ready to help the feeble of knee. He is the God blessed from everlasting to everlasting. Amen and hallelujah!

21

PSALM 107

Book V within the Psalms begins with number 107. This division, however, marks no break in the style of the Psalms. Like the ones immediately preceding, Psalm 107 is a praise psalm probably written after the exile for one of the annual festivals. Verse 3 pictures devotees streaming in from all directions, while the balance of the psalm features various hardships brought on by the dispersion. From each affliction God delivers the faithful.

The opening three verses are a kind of introductory summons to praise. Then follow four stanzas each dealing with a different kind of trouble. Verses 4-9 are about starving in the desert, verses 10-16 speak of imprisonment, verses 17-22 deal generally with sickness, and verses 23-32 describe the perils of sea travel. The last section, verses 33-43, constitutes a hymn of praise to God for His provisions which meet His people's needs.

Like Psalm 106:1 or 136:1, the opening words are typical of the Psalms. The word "covenant love," translated "mercy" (KJV, Anchor Bible), "lovingkindness" (ASV), and "steadfast love" (RSV), also appears in the refrains of verses 8, 15, 21, 31, and 43, the concluding verse of the psalm. Verse 2 is often quoted as an encouragement to witness. That is precisely its meaning here as well. Those worshipers gathered from around the Mediterranean were invited to share their testimonies of God's mercy and redemption.

The first category of hardship was desert wandering accompanied by hunger and thirst. In view of the fact that hundreds of miles of trackless wasteland separate Palestine from Babylonia and Assyria, some exiles may have suffered these very things journeying either as captives or pilgrims from one land to the other. Verse 6, like verses 13, 19, and 28 in the other stanzas, records their cry to God for help. God heard that cry and spared them. Then verse 8, with its wish form of the verb, urges men to praise God for His love and wonders (cf. vv. 15, 21, 31). To that refrain is added the reason for praise. It relates directly to the deliverance. According to verse 9, men should praise God because He fills and satisfies the hungry.

The second category of hardship is incarceration. The "shadow of death" found here in verses 10 and 14 is the same as that in Psalm 23:4. This confinement may refer to the actual treatment of captives by the Babylonian and Assyrian soldiers. However, the psalmist gives a spiritual reason for this particular punishment. They brought on this affliction through their rebellion against God and their scorn for His words (v. 11). Again, they cry for help and God spares them. It is interesting to note that spiritual salvation is often described as release from prison. In this connection compare Isaiah 42:7; 61:1; Psalm 102:20; Luke 1:79; 4: 18; 13:16; and 1 Peter 3:19.

Charles Wesley put it beautifully in his hymn, "And Can It Be That I Should Gain":

> Long my imprisoned spirit lay,
>   Fast bound in sin and nature's night;
> Thine eye diffused a quickening ray,
>   I woke, the dungeon flamed with light:
> My chains fell off, my heart was free,
>   I rose, went forth, and followed thee.

Verses 17 to 23 describe those with some debilitating disease which ruined their appetites. Healing for the malady is the "word" of God (v. 20). This may mean that God dispatched a specific order in response to their prayer, or that the Bible in general has the cure for the sin-sick soul.

"They that go down to the sea in ships" are the subjects of the last category (vv. 23-32). Throughout the Old Testament the Hebrews had little to do with the ocean. But though places such as Greece are connected by land to the Middle East, overland travel was virtually impossible because of international hostilities, lack of roads, danger of robbery, and general inconvenience. So God's people put to sea and exposed themselves to another set of difficulties and dangers. This, the longest of the four stanzas within this poem, describes a frightening, divinely sent storm and the resultant troubles for the sailors (vv. 25-27).

Once more the endangered prayed and once more the all-merciful God heard and saved. This theme too has occasioned Gospel songs and testimonies of salvation, for example, "Ship Ahoy!" "Let the Lower Lights Be Burning," and "Jesus, Saviour, Pilot Me."

The hymn at the close of Psalm 107 makes use of a series of contrasts. Note in verse 33 that God replaces deserts with rivers. Then verse 34 has the opposite. But verse 35 reverses the figures once more. Verses 36-38 describe the fortunes of the blessed, while verses 41 and 42 again underscore the benefits which come to the upright.

Verse 43 is a general conclusion to the poem and an exhortation to weigh and consider the varieties of God's faithful covenant love.

PSALM 108

Except for minor variations, the entirety of Psalm 108 is found elsewhere. The first five verses are nearly identical to Psalm 57:7-11 and the last seven verses are almost the same as Psalm 60:5-12. It is impossible to say which verses were written first. More comments than those found here appear under Psalms 57 and 60.

The brief title, "A Song, a Psalm of David," introduces this psalm. Three psalms in a row, beginning with this one, have ascriptions to David. Both Psalms 57 and 60 were ascribed to him, but with longer titles giving the occasions for the compositions.

The smaller opening portion (vv. 1-5) is purely praise. The psalmist testifies to his determination to sing and praise. Because of the reference to musical instruments, he may be leading a small orchestra or accompanying himself.

The parallelism is used rather strictly in verses 3 to 5. Note the synonymous pairs: give thanks—sing praises; peoples—nations; mercy—truth; heavens—skies; O God—Your glory.

Though this appears as a composite psalm, the two parts fit together very well. The opening Hebrew word translated "that" in verse 6 is, in fact, a kind of conjunction to introduce a resultant clause.

The word for "beloved" is essentially the same as the proper name David. To what extent David might have reminded God of the meaning of his name is just a guess.

This latter section is more of a prayer for military victory than praise. The title and context of Psalm 60 makes this even clearer. Apparently Israel had lost a battle and the people blamed themselves for faithlessness. This section of

Psalm 60 records God's words of threat against Israel's nearby foes. Actually, these words do not occur outside these two psalms. Gilead, Manasseh, and Ephraim all refer to the northern tribes, while Judah was the major tribe in the south. Moab and Edom were perennially hostile neighbors to the southeast, while Philistia constantly harassed Israel from the southwest.

Verses 11-13 are respectively complaint, prayer, and hope. To be cast off is to be abandoned to the enemy. If God should leave the army it cannot help but lose the battle, so the prayer is both a petition for help and a confession that no man can save. Although somewhat vengeful, the statement of faith in verse 13 speaks of profound conviction. The Jerusalem Bible paraphrase is worth noting: "With God among us, we shall fight like heroes."

PSALM 109

Psalm 109 illustrates the imprecatory psalms. Verses 6-19 are a series of curses invoked on an enemy. The opening five verses and the closing twelve frame this central section with the complaints, praises, and prayers of the psalmist.

One big question mark hangs over this psalm. Are the curses in verses 6-19 the words of David against his enemy or the words of the enemy against David? The first alternative is the more popular one. The translators of the Berkeley Bible even eliminate the option by adding the words "I pray" to verse 6. That way it certainly sounds like David's curse on his adversaries.

Several verses offer hints that the second alternative is correct. Verses 3 and 4 both mention the fact that the wicked have been accusing the righteous. So this may be the introduction to the long curse section. Also verse 20 mentions how the adversaries speak evil against the psalmist. Verse 28 has "Let them curse," which is exactly what they have been doing in the major part of the psalm.

If this latter interpretation is correct, then another problem is solved. The man of God is not as cruel, vengeful, and even caustic as it first appeared. These curses are not his words but his enemy's. The only imprecations coming directly from the God-fearer are the two relatively mild ones of verse 29. On the other hand, David and other Old Testament saints were not above heaping curses on their foes. Psalms 69, 137, and 143 all contain unabashed imprecations.

The entire psalm has overtones of a court scene. The plaintiff is the psalmist and gathered around to accuse him are false witnesses (v. 3), a corrupt jury (v. 5), and a judge open to bribery (vv. 6-7). Under those circumstances the righteous man has only one source of help: God. So the opening words of the psalm are a desperate prayer that God, the key Witness against the trumped-up charges, will speak up. Notice that one facet of the complaint is the assertion of personal innocence. And not only that, but while they hated, he loved; while they cursed, he prayed (vv. 4-5). Think of Jesus' words in Matthew 5:44, "Pray for them which despitefully use you."

The central portion of the psalm (vv. 6-19) contains some of the most vituperative, invective, and vitriolic vengeance found anywhere in Scripture. The word pictures are vivid and cruel. Verses 6 and 7 describe the legal process of accusation. The King James Version and the Anchor Bible both transliterate the Hebrew word for "accuser" into the proper name "Satan." The latter version reads in the first line, "Evil One," thus making it too a title for the enemy of all righteous men. The root for the word "accuse" (Heb., *satan*) occurs also in verses 4, 20, and 29 ("adversaries" in KJV and ASV).

The next curse is a wish for the adversaries' death (v. 8). The latter half of this verse, along with Psalm 69:25, is cited in Acts 1:20 in connection with Judas Iscariot's suicide. The consequences of such an early death would mean a widowed wife, fatherless children, and a destitute situation for all.

Verses 11 and 12 expand on that theme of financial stress which verse 10 introduced. The prayer is that the creditors will demand and extract in payment all his savings and that strangers will enjoy the things he worked for so long.

The maledictions of verses 12 and 13 continue even to the dead man's offspring (picking up the theme of vv. 9-10). He wishes for them, as well, to die so that there will be no memory of the cursed man after one brief generation. This evil wish shows something of how some ancient people thought of life after death. They believed that a man lives only in the minds of those who work at remembering him (cf. v. 15). It certainly is a sub-Christian view, but it is still maintained by many modern Jews, especially of the reformed movement.

Verses 14 and 15, on the other hand, envision a divine judgment after death. The curser prays that the man might also be charged with his parents' sins (cf. Num 14:18).

The curse wishes break off at verse 16 for three verses in order to enumerate the reasons for the charges. This man, be he the psalmist's enemy in the usual interpretation, or the psalmist in the interpretation I favor, is charged rightly or wrongly with unkindness, cruelty, murder, and cursing. The

28

imagery of verse 18 may relate to the water ordeal of Numbers 5:22.

The final verse in this section, 19, reverts to the jussive or wish form of the verb to wrap up the victim in the very curses with which he chose to clothe himself.

The third major part of the psalm begins with verse 20. No one questions that these words are the psalmist's and not a quotation of someone else. He and not the wicked accuser is more likely to appear to the Lord. So verse 20 is the transition from the imprecations to the complaints. Verse 21 is a prayer with typical "riders" on it to help make God feel His responsibility. This ancient saint tacks on the "for Your name's sake" argument (Amp.) and the phrase "in the goodness of thy unfailing love" (NEB). What can God do but respond positively!

Protestations of helplessness fill verses 22 through 25. Count the first person pronouns there: I am weak. I am needy. I am like a shadow or a locust. My heart is sick. My knees are weak. My body is gaunt.

The words of this suffering servant in verse 25 find an echo in the crucifixion accounts of Matthew (27:39) and Mark (15:29). At that scene also men shook their heads at the accused.

Verse 28 might be a good thought to keep in mind when one is personally vilified. It predates considerably the words of Jesus in Matthew 5:44 and Luke 6:28 and the injunction of Paul in Romans 12:14. Our Lord said, "Bless them that curse you," and the apostle Paul said, "Bless, and curse not."

As noted above, verse 29 may be the only real imprecation from the mouth of the psalmist. By comparison with verses 6-19 it is kind, but notice that the same figure of a garment is used (cf. vv. 18-19).

The final two verses are praise and assertion. Just as

29

Psalm 108 closed with an expressed confidence in the ultimate justice of God, so this one ends on a note of assurance that the virtuous will be acquitted and exonerated because of a just God who stands by the side of the accused. Observe how many of the terms in the opening verses are repeated at the close: mouth, praise, stand, right hand, and condemn. At the beginning it was a kind of kangaroo court, but in the end the Judge of all the earth effects justice.

PSALM 110

Psalm 110 is the most popular of the Messianic psalms. Quotations from it and allusions to it occur more than twenty times in the New Testament. This is remarkable in view of its seven brief verses. Jesus Himself used the first verse to prove His deity (Mt 22:44; Mk 12:36; Lk 20:42-43). Peter cited it in Acts 2:34 when he preached at Pentecost, and the author of Hebrews quoted it at 1:13. In addition, the concept of Christ sitting at the right hand of God appears many times (Mt 26:64; Mk 14:62; 16:19; Lk 22:69; Eph 1:20; Col 3:1; Heb 1:3; 8:1; 10:12; 12:2; and 1 Pe 3:22). Also the idea of the enemies being a footstool occurs in 1 Corinthians 15:25; Ephesians 1:22; and Hebrews 10:13.

The Hebrews author quotes and refers to verse 4 as well. (See Heb 5:6, 10; 6:20; 7:11, 15, 17, 21.) These inspired comments by Christ and the apostles should be adequate to guarantee the Messianic character of this psalm.

As to its structure, Psalm 110 also proves intriguing. There is a parallel between verses 1 and 5, 2 and 6, 3 and 7. Notice the words "right hand" in the first pair; the synonyms, "enemies," "nations," and "countries," in the second pair; and the ideas of moisture, "dew" and "brook," in the third pair (ASV).

Furthermore, note that verses 1 and 7 speak of opposites, "feet" and "head," while verses 3 and 5 both mention the day God goes to war. "Day of power" is in verse 3 and "day of wrath" in verse 5 (NASB).

All this leaves the middle verse, 4, unconnected. This statement certainly is the apex of the psalm. While verse 1 may speak of the royal prerogatives of the Messiah, verse 4 states His priestly office and lineage.

Despite the usual English translations, the verb "said" in verse 1 really represents a much stronger action such as oracle or divine pronouncement (cf. The Jerusalem Bible and Anchor Bible). Therefore, it balances well with the strong thought of verse 4a: "The LORD hath sworn and will not repent."

Now let us examine the composition verse by verse. The title ascribes the psalm to David, and the words of Christ in Matthew 22:44 agree to this. The fact that David wrote it is part of the argument. How can the Messiah be merely David's son if David himself called Him "Lord"?

Most English versions note when God's proper Hebrew name is used by spelling LORD with all capital letters. The American Standard Version renders the name "Jehovah" and The Jerusalem Bible, "Yahweh." Unless this distinction is clear, verse 1 makes little sense. But here God the Father is addressing God the Son and granting Him the honored position on the right hand.

So far the poem could be a royal psalm, since David the king did enjoy certain privileges as God's favorite earthly monarch. The vowels in the Hebrew expression for "my lord," which the Jewish scribes put in, indicate a human title,

31

but the inspired consonantal text would allow either human or divine.

Verse 2 speaks of the Lord delegating authority to the Son. From Zion, the poetic name for Jerusalem, Christ's rule will go out and ultimately bring even His enemies into submission. Philippians 2:10-11 comes to mind, that every knee shall bow to the name of Jesus and every tongue shall confess that Jesus Christ is Lord. This verse also echoes Psalm 2:9, which speaks of the Messiah's conquest of all unsubmissive powers.

The first half of verse 3 shows Christ's army ready and willing to fight on the chosen day. The Revised Standard Version, The Jersualem Bible, and other versions, together with several Hebrew manuscripts use the phrase "on the holy mountains" instead of "in holy array" (ASV), or the like. The two words would be very similar in the original language. The holy mountains then would be the hills around Jerusalem, including Mount Zion.

Difficult indeed is the last half of verse 3. The words are all readable but the figure of speech is strange. The phrase may refer to the vigor and virility of the conquering Messiah.

The high point of the psalm is verse 4. God the Father puts Himself under an irrevocable oath that the Messiah is indeed a Priest. He is not a Levitical priest but a Melchizedek Priest. In the Epistle to the Hebrews much is made of this unique analogy between Christ and the ancient king of Salem. Genesis 14 is the record on which this verse is based. After routing a Mesopotamian coalition, Abraham gave a tithe to this otherwise unknown king-priest, Melchizedek. The point of chapters 5 to 7 of the book of Hebrews is that Christ is of a superior, more ancient line of priests. As royalty He is from the tribe of Judah (Heb 7:14), but as a priest He is not from the tribe of Levi (Heb 7:11-13). Melchizedek preceded Levi just as Christ is a Priest distinct from and better than the Levites (Heb 7:22-24).

Verse 5 begins the anticlimax in the second half of the chiastic outline of this psalm. Many of the elements in verses 5-7 reflect or echo words and ideas in the first half of David's composition. A minor problem exists in the opening line. The Berkeley and New American Standard Bibles solve it by reading the divine name (YHWH) "LORD" instead of the usual "Lord." The question is: Is this God the Father or the Son? If He is the Father how can He be at the right hand of the Son, since verse 1 showed it the other way around? If He is the Son, then there is a change of addressee. Up till now the "you" (or "thou") has referred to the Son, not the Father. The former explanation is preferable, that it is God the Father at the right hand of the Son (despite the logistics problem) helping Him win in the day of battle.

In verse 6 is a description of the judging-destroying process. Again, all the words are clear, but how to put them together has been a problem for all Bible students. A casual glance at several modern versions will show the different possibilities. Whatever the exact meaning is, the general thrust of the passage is Christ's victory over His foes.

If the interpretation of other verses has been in doubt, the last one certainly is obscure. All the Hebrew words appear to be intact, but to make sense of the picture or figure of speech is very hard. Since verse 7 has some structural connection with verse 3b, the phrases might refer to the victorious Hero refreshing Himself after the heat of the battle has passed.

Altogether this is a most fascinating, interesting, and important psalm. Though it is short and despite its difficulties, it deserves much study, especially because the New Testament writers used it so extensively to argue the case for the kingship and high priesthood of the Lord Jesus Christ.

PSALM 111

After the initial hallelujah (Hebrew for "Praise the LORD"). Psalm 111 is a perfect alphabetic acrostic. Each of the twenty-two lines (two in each verse except verses 9 and 10, which have three each) begins with the successive letter of the Hebrew alphabet. Some Bibles list these Hebrew letters at Psalm 119, the most outstanding of the acrostics in the Psalter. Other alphabetic acrostics are Psalms 9 and 10 together, 25, 34, 37, 112, and 145.

In addition to Psalms 111 and 119, several sections outside the book of Psalms also follow an acrostic pattern. They are Proverbs 31:10-31; Lamentations 1, 2, 3, and 4; and Nahum 1. Since there are twenty-two letters in the Hebrew alphabet, note how many of these passages have multiples of twenty-two in the number of their lines.

Psalms 111 and 112 represent the simplest system with just one line for each letter. Lamentations 4 has two lines for each letter, Lamentations 1, 2, and 3 have three lines for each letter, and Psalm 119 has eight lines for each letter.

It may be that the author of this psalm was so concerned with his alphabetic scheme that he did not work too hard on the contiguity of the whole. In general it is a praise psalm, but there are no specific references to people, places, or times, so the occasion for its composition is unknown. From a grammatical point of view the Hebrew word order is often unusual. The effort to fit the poem into the acrostic system has undoubtedly occasioned this.

The psalmist mostly speaks of praising God for His many benefits to His people. The only "I" is at verse 1. Otherwise all the attention is on what God has done.

The first adjectives are very general: the works of the Lord are great and desirable (v. 2). With verses 3 and 4 (RSV) more specific terms appear: honor, majesty, righteousness, grace, and mercy. Even more specificity comes with verse 5: God gives food and remembers His covenant. Although some commentators see this as a reference to the manna in the wilderness, it is an unusual word with the basic meaning of "victim" or "prey." Perhaps verse 5a is to be understood with verse 6b, so that the prey is the land of Canaan which God gave to Israel.

If there is any division to the psalm, it comes between verses 5 and 6. There are broad comparisons between the two halves of the work. Note the linking words "the congregation" and "his people" (vv. 1, 6); "the works of the LORD" and "the works of his hands" (vv. 2, 7); "for ever" (vv. 3, 8); "his covenant" (vv. 5, 9); and "fear" (vv. 5, 10).

The items for praise continue through the second half of the psalm in most general terms. Proverbs 1:7 and 9:10 reflect the opening line of verse 10: "The fear of the LORD is the beginning of wisdom."

PSALM 112

Like Psalm 111, Psalm 112 is an alphabetic acrostic. And like Psalm 111 it has its twenty-two lines in ten verses (the last two verses using the last six letters of the Hebrew alphabet). Both psalms begin with a hallelujah. For these rea-

sons, plus many other similarities in vocabulary, most Bible
students attribute these two poems to the same inspired, although anonymous, author.

Whereas Psalm 111 was a hymn of praise to God for His
goodness, Psalm 112 speaks of the blessed way of life the
godly man has. Several of the virtues attributed to God in
Psalm 111 describe the righteous man in Psalm 112. Note
righteousness (111:3; 112:3), grace and mercy (111:4;
112:4), and honor (111:3; 112:9).

There is also a connection between the last verse of Psalm
111 and the opening one of this psalm. Blessed is that man
who fears the LORD because he has begun to be wise. Also
note that idea in Psalm 111:5. The word "command" also
ties 111:9 to 112:1.

With verse 1*b* we have an answer to the question: What
does it mean to fear God? It means to delight to obey His
commandments. The "commandments" are not limited to
the famous ten or even to the legal portions of the Old Testament, but to all teaching about God. Psalm 119 is an extended treatment of the same theme.

Verse 2 begins a list of the benefits that accrue to such
a good man. Most of the success is measured in rather mate-
rialistic terms, but the authors of the psalms did not have
the teaching of Christ to guide them. They operated under
the belief that the good are rewarded with money and health
while the wicked suffer shame and sickness. We know that
wealth can be counted in ways other than money and that
blessings come in many unostentatious forms.

The miscellaneous thoughts continue, hitting on certain
traits and characteristics of the good man. Like God, he is
gracious, merciful, and righteous—three of the communicable attributes (v. 4*b*). The attitude of generosity comes

up in both verses 5 and 9. Incidentally, Paul cites verse 9 in 2 Corinthians 9:9.

A good reputation, even after death, was a coveted thing. Verses 2 and 6 mention that. Note also that verses 3 and 9 end on the same theme.

Because this saintly believer fears the Lord (v. 1), he will not be afraid of bad news (v. 7) or have a fearful heart (v. 8). The exact meaning of verse 8b is uncertain. Most translations either add a word such as "his desire" (KJV, ASV, RSV) or strengthen the word "see" into "gloat over" (NEB) or "looks down upon" (NAB). The Berkeley Version, however, avoids both these solutions by simply reading: "He will be joyful and unafraid, while he looks upon his adversaries."

Perhaps a comment is in order about the "horn" of verse 9. This meaningful word has a much broader sense than its usual connotation. It not only represents that bony growth on an animal's head which is occasionally made into a musical instrument, but in the Bible it also stands for strength (Dan 8:3-9), fertility (Is 5:1), or supernatural office (Ex 34:29).

The foes who were mentioned in verse 8 are the entire subject of verse 10. Because of their envy of God's blessing on the righteous, they grieve, curse themselves, and despair. The terms the psalmist chose, especially "gnash with his teeth," were probably common ways to express this almost neurotic surrender of hope. In order not to end up in that wretched psychological state, we need to revere the Lord and find joy in His Word.

37

PSALM 113

As part of the Jewish liturgy for Passover, Psalms 113-18 are sung. This may be the "hymn" that Jesus and His disciples sang after the Last Supper (Mt 26:30). Notice that Psalm 113 both begins and ends with a hallelujah or "Praise the LORD." The Greek translation, however, which several modern versions follow, puts the latter hallelujah at the beginning of Psalm 114. This is also done in Psalms 115, 116, and 117 so that all the psalms in the group from 111 to 118, with the exception of 115, begin with hallelujah.

This brief hymn of praise divides neatly into three stanzas of three verses each. Excluding the hallelujahs, within each verse are two stichs. The first third of the poem speaks of the greatness of God's name. The second portion focuses on God's transcendence. And the third part stresses God's concern for affairs on earth.

Verse 1 is a general summons to God's people to praise Him. Then verse 2 speaks of the temporal extent of that praise, and verse 3 tells the geographical extent. God's name is blessed at all times and in all places. Notice the chiastic arrangement of verses 2 and 3. The first and the fourth elements are parallel and the two interior elements are parallel.

    A   May the LORD's name be blessed
        B   From now to eternity
        B'   From east to west
    A'   May the LORD's name be praised.

The middle group of verses affirms God's position above both the earth and the heavens. Everything is clear until verse 6, which can be translated several ways but with little variation in basic meaning. It may mean that God is so high above heaven and earth that He must stoop even to see them. Or it may say that this great God is, in fact, concerned with all the details of His creation, heaven and earth included. A glance at the translations will show how these different interpretations are worded.

The last three verses portray vividly the compassionate interest God has in the unfortunate. It is He who reverses fortunes, taking a man from the dung heap to the throne room. It is He who blesses otherwise barren women with babies. Because He is so lofty and because He is so near, praise the Lord.

PSALM 114

Included in Psalm 114 are a couple of the more picturesque figures of speech in the Hebrew Bible. No one can visualize the mountains and hills skipping about like rams and lambs, but such is the figure the psalmist chose to describe either the Sinai earthquake or the conquest of Canaan.

The theme of Psalm 114 is God's deliverance of Israel out of Egypt and into the promised land. If the translation of the opening word is "after" rather than "when," the anachronism of verse 2 is eliminated. The very mention of Judah and Israel implies knowledge of the divided kingdom which existed from the death of Solomon (922 B.C.) to the Assyrian conquest of Samaria (722 B.C.). The Exodus from Egypt occurred several hundred years before Solomon.

Only one other problem attends this psalm. The last word of verse 1 is quite uncertain. Based on postbiblical Hebrew and other cognate languages, the interpretation has been "strange language." But the word may also be read as "strong" or "cruel." Compare Isaiah 25:3 where the same words occur. Such a rereading does not affect the overall interpretation.

The four middle verses state some facts concerning the Exodus and then ask questions about those facts. The sea which looked and fled was, of course, the Red Sea. Exodus 14:21-22 records that event. The Jordan also turned back as the Israelites began their assault on the west bank. Joshua 3:14-16 records that event.

If the quaking of the mountains refers to the phenomena surrounding the giving of the Law on Sinai, it is chronologically out of order in this psalm. Others see it as a figurative way to describe the conquest of Canaan and, in particular, the miraculous overthrow of the walls of Jericho.

The answer to the questions of verses 5 and 6 is the power of God, who works on behalf of His people.

Notice in verse 7, as elsewhere in this psalm, the use of staircase parallelism. The element "at the presence of God" is shared by both lines. But the first line begins with a verb, understood only in the second line. The second line modifies God's name to include Jacob. This longer title for God can be implied in the first line. So the lines are parallel, but each has something the other does not have and they balance. Verses 1 and 4 evidence the same feature.

The last of the Exodus miracles alluded to in this psalm is the water from the rock at Meribah (Ex 17:6-7; Num 20:11-13). Because of the strong emphasis this psalm puts on the Exodus, it is understandable why the Hebrews use it as part of the Passover ritual.

PSALM 115

The contrast between the living, creating God of Israel and the powerless, inanimate idols of the heathen is the subject of Psalm 115. Sections of the psalm sound liturgical. The repetitious series in verses 9-11 and 12 and 13 point in that direction.

The opening verse is a general introductory praise note. Two of God's outstanding attributes, mercy and truth, are underscored. The first of these, especially, represents a whole series of virtues that "mercy" only begins to name. The Hebrew word also means loving-kindness, covenant love, steadfastness, integrity, fidelity, and promise-keeping.

A question comes from the mouths of the unbelieving Gentiles: Where is their God? Perhaps it was a real question. After all, there were no statues of Yahweh, the God of the Hebrews, and to this day no archaeological excavation has produced one. Those heathen, just like the ones today, had difficulty even imagining, much less worshiping, a God of spirit and truth.

Verse 3 gives the answer. God is in heaven, not in the shape of a statue. Then begins a mockery of the whole system of idolatry. Only Isaiah (44:9-20) is more pungent in his satire on images. Whereas the God of Israel does or makes whatever He pleases, these pagan gods are man-made (v. 4).

In verses 5-7 there is a list of inadequacies. Though the images appear to have all their faculties—mouths, eyes, ears, noses, hands, feet, and throats—all are inoperative. Nothing works. All is for show alone.

The first part of the psalm ends on the caustic indictment

that idolaters will be just like the idols they worship, namely, dead.

With verse 9 begins a section that may have been sung antiphonally. It is quite possible that a soloist, perhaps a senior priest, sang the first half of each verse and that the choir sang the response: "He is their help and shield." "Shield" as a title for God goes back to Genesis 15:1 where God promised Abraham, "I am thy shield and thy exceeding great reward."

This group of three verses (9-11) is very similar to Psalm 135:19-20. Some think there were three distinct categories of worshipers corresponding to the three courtyards in the later Temple of Herod: the priests (house of Aaron), the Jews at large (house of Israel), and the converts (you that fear the LORD). Note how the three categories of worshipers appear again in the threefold benediction of verses 12 and 13.

From the central part of the psalm the focus turns once more to the character and attributes of God. He alone gives increase (v. 14). He made heaven and earth (v. 15). He receives no praise from dead men (v. 17).

Some sciolistic Bible students have singled out verse 16 as a condemnation of modern space travel. The verse speaks to God's sovereign, creative power, not to who belongs where. If they are correct and man has no right to the sky then, conversely, God has no right on earth, which is simply not true.

Verse 17 reflects some of the pre-New Testament thinking regarding the afterlife. From the psalmist's limited perspective, death ends all participation at the sanctuary. Likewise, the ineffective service of idolaters to lifeless gods produces no praise from the true and living God.

Only the people who can sing this psalm are able to bless

the Lord. And to that end they pledged themselves by aver-ring their intentions in the closing verse of Psalm 115.

PSALM 116

In the Greek and Latin Bibles, Psalm 116 is counted as two psalms with the break after verse 9. Both halves are a testimony to God's faithfulness through a time of sickness. Note the similarity of verses 1-4 to verses 10-11. Then verses 5-9 and 12-19 are roughly parallel in their words of praise and promise.

Although the opening words may sound somewhat com-mercial, it is true that we cannot outdo God in love. We only love Him because He loved us first. His love to us is not prompted by our affection or obedience but by His own di-vine character. In particular, the author of this psalm is grateful to be alive. Over and over, this theme appears throughout the psalm. If verse 3 were in our idiom, it would be, "I was at death's door" rather than "the cords of death encompassed me."

The dire circumstances prompted a personal prayer for deliverance and health. Some Bible students see similarities between this prayer, and the one of King Hezekiah when he too was near death (Is 38:10-20).

Notice the figures of speech in the testimony of salvation (vv. 5-9). God delivered the psalmist's soul, perhaps saved his breath, spared his eyes from tears, and kept his feet from slipping. Then he picks up the idea of the feet to state in verse 9 that he will walk before the Lord in the land of the living.

As Hebrew poetry this psalm has some unusual forms, so the sense of the first line of verse 10 may be, "I believe and certainly will speak." By revocalizing the second verb, the Anchor Bible offers, "I remained faithful though I was pursued."

Verse 11 has the rather nasty remark that "all men are liars." Since this is the only time in the Bible the word in question occurs in this form, perhaps a milder sense is correct. The Revised Standard Version has "Men are all a vain hope," while Moffatt suggests, "All men are a failure."

The balance of the psalm is filled with promises of service and devotion. Only verse 15, a familiar one, interrupts the series. Here are some of the psalmist's "renderings" (v. 12) to the Lord for His benefits. He says in verse 13 that he will take the cup of salvation, a very beautiful picture in itself (cf. Ps 23:5b). He will call on God's name (vv. 13, 17b). He will pay his vows (vv. 14, 18). He confesses his servant role (v. 16), and he will offer sacrifices of thanksgiving in the public courts of God's house in Jerusalem (vv. 14, 18, 19).

Now what does verse 15 mean? Often it is cited in connection with martyrs who die for their faith. Sometimes we hear it quoted at the funerals of faithful Christians, especially if they are elderly. The meaning of all the Hebrew words is clear, but the meaning of the entire verse is difficult. Can it mean that God is anxious to see His followers die? Or does He hate to see them die? How can death be described as precious? Most likely the real meaning lies close to all the suggestions in this paragraph. It is no small concern to God. He, like the apostle Paul and us, must have mixed feelings about the death of godly people (cf. Phil 1:23). To die and be with God in person will be sheer bliss. To live and serve is privilege and duty. The verse simply underscores, from God's perspective, the importance of this event which ushers the saint from a life of sickness, servitude, and struggle to one of relief, release, and rejoicing. Is it not comforting to know that God is more concerned with our death than we are?

PSALM 117

As is commonly known, Psalm 117 is the shortest chapter in the Bible. Coincidentally, it comes two chapters before the longest, which is Psalm 119. Furthermore, it is the middle chapter of the Bible with 594 preceding it and 594 following. Cardinal Hugo de Sancto Caro divided the Bible into chapters in the year 1250, and we do not know if he planned it this way or not. Such a phenomenon certainly should not be used as a proof for inspiration or the like.

Psalm 117 is a summons to all nations to praise the Lord. Notice the chiasmus with the opening and closing words "Praise the LORD."

Two attributes are singled out—God's mercy and truth. Psalm 115:1 mentioned the same two characteristics of the Deity. The first one, in particular, is a rich word carrying the basic meaning of faithfulness to covenant promise. Each attribute is also modified with an adjective. His loving-kindness is great and His truth is everlasting. Hallelujah!

PSALM 118

Psalm 118 is a hymn of thanksgiving to the Lord for salvation. While a particular military victory may have occasioned its composition, the terms are very general and can refer to all sorts of divine deliverance, physical and spiritual.

Several verses in the psalm are familiar because they appear in the New Testament. Matthew (21:42) and Mark (12:10-11) quote both verses 22 and 23, while Luke (20: 17) and Peter (1 Pe 2:7) use only verse 22. Luke, in Acts 4:11, again alludes to the figure of the rejected stone.

All four evangelists cite verses 25-26 in their passion narratives. (See Mt 21:9; 23:39; Mk 11:9-10; Lk 13:35; 19: 38; Jn 12:13.) In addition, verse 6 appears in Hebrews 13:6.

Some scholars see similarities between this psalm and the song of Moses in Exodus 15. Compare verses 14 and 28 with Exodus 15:2 and verses 15 and 16 with Exodus 15:6. Because of this, some date Psalm 118 early while others, noting the allusion to the Temple (e.g., v. 26), date it later.

Several obvious changes in subject matter divide the poem into several parts. Verses 1-4 constitute an invitation to praise. Next follow three sections (vv. 5-9, 10-12, 13-18) which speak of God's deliverance from trouble, hostilities, and death. Verses 19-29 read like a Temple liturgy with at least two speakers. One is the priest who allows only the righteous to enter the Temple. The other is the psalmist who himself enters and worships.

The use of repetition is quite remarkable throughout this psalm. The opening and closing verses are identical. The same refrain as in those two appears in verses 2, 3, and 4. Verses 6 and 7 open the same way. Except for the last words (in Hebrew) of verses 8 and 9, these two are identical. The last stichs of verses 10, 11, and 12 match, as well as the verbs in the first stichs. The expression "the right hand of the LORD" is used three times in verses 15 and 16. Both "gate" and "righteous" are in verses 19 and 20.

After the theme verse (1) which begins and ends the

psalm, there is a threefold invitation to reflect God's mercy. The house of Israel, the house of Aaron, and those who fear the Lord represent the Jewish laity, the clergy, and the converts, respectively. Once more the most notable attribute receives the focus. The phrase "His mercy endures forever" occurs five times in this psalm but twenty-six times in Psalm 136. The Hebrew word is *hesed* and the fullest meaning is "faithfulness to covenant promise." Since God promised love, mercy, and kindness, various translations use one or more of these for their interpretation of this very full term.

The nature of the trouble mentioned in verse 5 is unknown. Most likely it had to do with military confrontation, and the psalmist is speaking in the first person for the entire nation. Notice the contrast between the "tight spot" ("distress") and the "open space" in verse 5, a vivid way of expressing trouble and release. The next four verses are two pairs. Because the Lord is on the side of the righteous, they need not fear human enemies. Compare the remarks on Psalm 112:8 regarding the elliptical phrase at the end of verse 7.

It is not bad or wrong to trust men; it is just better to trust the Lord. People fail. Governments wane. Weapons prove inadequate. But God never fails.

The verb "cut down" or "cut off" appears three times in verses 10-12 (RSV). Everywhere but here and in Psalms 90:6 and 58:7 it means circumcise. However, the form of the verb is unique to these three verses.

Some Bible translators avoid the question of the addressee in verse 13 by choosing not to read the Hebrew but some other ancient version. It cannot be God who tries to trip up the believer. He is mentioned in the third person in the same verse. Perhaps it is death personified (cf. v. 18). Whoever that enemy was, God proved Himself the strong Saviour.

47

The voice of rejoicing sings three tributes to the right hand of God (vv. 15-16). As with us, the right hand is the position and sign of favor and blessing (cf. Ps 110:1). Rodin the sculptor did the hand of God—it is a right hand. He also carved the hand of Satan—it is a left hand. When Rembrandt painted Jeremiah bemoaning the destruction of Jerusalem, only the prophet's left hand and foot appear—a symbol of the unhappy, unfortunate, inauspicious events of the exile.

Verses 19 and 20 read like a conversation at the Temple gate. First the worshiper asks entrance. Then the gatekeeper cites the qualifications for entrance (cf. Ps 15).

The circumstances which prompted verse 22 are uncertain. It is possible there was a prominent stone rejected by the masons that eventually became the cornerstone. In any event, the New Testament writers apply this to Christ, who indeed was rejected by many only to become the cornerstone of the Church (cf. Eph 2:20).

Likewise, the occasion behind verses 25 and 26 is not known. Perhaps these verses were sung in connection with pilgrims making their way to the annual festivals in Jerusalem. The Hebrew words for "save now" are approximately *hosan na*. We know, of course, that the most significant Person to make His way to the Temple was the Lord Jesus Christ, the Messiah Himself.

Many Bible students continue to have the Messiah in mind as they read verse 27. Hence they see Christ, the Lamb of God, as the sacrifice bound to the horns of the altar.

The psalm ends with notes of praise, thanksgiving, and exaltation.

PSALM 119

Psalm 119 is outstanding in several ways. It is the longest psalm and the longest chapter in the Bible. Its 176 verses are almost double the next longest chapter, Numbers 7 with its eighty-nine verses. Psalm 119 is two chapters away from the middle chapter of the Bible, Psalm 117.

The 176 verses are divided into twenty-two groups or stanzas of eight verses. Each of the eight verses within a stanza begins with the same letter of the Hebrew alphabet. In this way each of those twenty-two letters begins eight consecutive verses. The letters are in alphabetical order. Some editions of the English Bible have the Hebrew letters printed, others have the name of the letter written out at the head of each stanza. Hence verses 1-8 all begin with *aleph,* verses 9-16 with *beth,* verses 17-24 with *gimel,* and so on to the end of the psalm.

Of the 176 verses, 114 are found completely or in part in one of the Dead Sea Scrolls. This helps in those few places where there are textual problems.

The psalm is a magnificent hymn of praise about God's Word. Synonyms for the Bible appear in every verse except verse 122. (Four other verses, 84, 90, 121, and 132, are questionable.) But several verses have two epithets for Scripture, for example, 43, 48, and 160. Some of these terms are: law, testimony, way, precept, statute, command, ordinance, and word.

Although no New Testament author quotes from Psalm 119 (with the possible exception of verse 139 in John 2:17, but cf. Ps 69:9), several of its verses are very familiar, even from childhood. Verse 9 is:

> How shall a young man cleanse his way?
> By taking heed . . . to thy word.

Verse 11 has:

> Thy word have I hid in mine heart
> That I might not sin against thee.

And verse 105 (NASB) reads:

> Thy word is a lamp to my feet,
> And a light to my path.

Naturally, with the main focus on the Word of God, there are many affirmations about its truthfulness, its endurance, and its benefactions. Verse 89 stresses its immutability:

> For ever, O LORD,
> Thy word is settled in heaven.

Verse 160 (ASV) underscores its veracity and eternality:

> The sum of thy word is truth;
> And every one of thy righteous ordinances endureth forever.

Verses 99 and 165 record its advantages:

> I have more understanding than all my teachers.
> Great peace have they that love thy law.

Scholars debate whether or not there is any overall outline to the psalm. Some see a more or less miscellaneous collection of ideas focused on the characteristics of the Law of the Lord and the psalmist's attitude toward it. It is wisdom literature akin to the Proverbs. Others struggle to outline the poem and fit titles to each group of eight verses. This latter approach is unconvincing.

There are ten synonyms for the Word of God. This has prompted some Bible students to match them up with the

Ten Commandments. Others count only eight different terms and assume that the writer wanted to use each one but once in each stanza. This obviously was not the case, and to make it work would require severe emendation.

A number of verses hint that the author was the victim of either some disease (e.g., vv. 25, 50, 75, 83, 143) or of some persecution (e.g., vv. 53, 61, 69-71, 78, 141). The prayer "quicken me" occurs over and over (e.g., vv. 25, 40, 88, 107, 149, 154, 159). This too may show the bad health or the dangerous situation of the psalm's author. Otherwise, clues to who wrote it are unavailable. Some say he was old and near death because of the other reasons, while others say he was a young man because of such statements as: "I have more understanding than all my teachers" (v. 99), or "I understand more than the aged" (v. 100, ASV).

One thing is certain, the author loves the Word of God. In fact, one of his verses that has been put to music is 97:

> O how love I thy law!
> It is my meditation all the day.

Verse 11, cited above, is also a well-known Gospel song.

Rather than proceed through the psalm verse by verse, this study focuses on the different titles for God's Word.

1. Law. This is the Hebrew word *torah*. Basically the meaning is "that which is given out," hence, taught. It refers not merely to the Decalogue or to the Pentateuch but to the entire corpus of information God has given. It occurs in verse 1 and in twenty-four other places in Psalm 119.

2. Testimonies. This word refers to God's statement about Himself and the world in general. The term describes the Ark of the Covenant in the tabernacle and later in the Temple, and the tablets of the Ten Commandments kept in the Ark. Overtones of the legal system are here as well as in

51

the other synonyms. His testimonies are His record of the things He knows to be true. Variations of the root appear in verse 2 and in twenty-two others places in the psalm.

3. "Way" translates two different Hebrew words. The one used in verses 3, 14, 27, 30, 32, 33, and 37 is the usual word. It means everything from a path to a highway.

4. The second word for "way" is behind the translation in verse 15. It comes up several other times but not as a synonym of Scripture.

5. Of the twenty-four occurrences of the word "precepts" in the Bible, twenty-one are in Psalm 119. This is a suitable translation, the only other good option being "charge."

6. In verse 5, and twenty other times, we read the word "statutes." This term has the force of an inscribed royal decree. In the Pentateuch it is often coupled with one of the other words in this list, usually "commandment." As in our legal system, it is a more particularized legal requirement rather than a broad statement demanding good behavior.

7. "Command" or "commandment" occurs twenty-two times in the psalm. Even though this is the number of stanzas, its appearances are not distributed one to each stanza. This Hebrew word is widely known in English as the second element in the expression Bar Mitzvah, literally "son of a command," meaning a boy now old enough to be responsible. Interestingly, this word does not describe the Decalogue in Hebrew. They are called the "ten words" (Ex 34:28; Deu 4:13; 10:4).

8. "Judgments" (usually KJV), or "ordinances" (usually ASV, RSV, and others), or "rulings" (usually JB), appears nineteen times in Psalm 119. As the various alternatives indicate, the word does not necessarily imply a judicial verdict of guilty. As well, it might mean exoneration or acquittal. A judge in ancient Israel was a leader, often charismatic and

52

military, who, among many other things, adjudicated disputes.

9. The most common term for "word" in Hebrew is *dabar*. With its cognates (e.g., the verbal form *speak*), it is the most frequently used word in the language. In Psalm 119 it is used twenty-two times (but again, not evenly distributed). Both the singular and the plural occur. Once (v. 43) it is in the construction, "word of truth."

10. A less frequent term translated "word" or "promise" occurs nineteen times in this psalm. These represent over half the total in the Old Testament. It is related to a very common verb (*say*) and may have in it the idea of the spoken word.

Just as a reading of Psalm 119 may seem endless, so our praise for God and His Word should be endless. From a New Testament perspective the Word is also the incarnate Christ. To read this psalm with the Lord Jesus in mind, or, even to use His name in place of the various names for the Bible, makes a very rich devotional experience. Verse 162 is a random example of this exercise. It also brings to mind the parable of the pearl of great price (Mt 13:45-46).

> I rejoice in the Lord Jesus Christ
> As one that finds great spoil.

Another would be verse 173:

> Let Your hand be ready to help me
> Because I have chosen Jesus Christ.

Try it!

Psalms 120 through 134 all have the title "a song of ascents" or degrees. Most Bible students connect this term with the ascent to Jerusalem for the annual festivals: Passover, Pentecost, and the Feast of Tabernacles. The pilgrims sang these psalms as they went (Ex 23:14; Deu 16:16; Lk 2:41-42). Jerusalem is on a hill, but by no means a high one. In fact, the adjacent Mount of Olives raises one hundred feet higher than the holy city itself. But because of its religious significance, Jerusalem is the highest mountain in the world.

Less popular suggestions concerning the "song of ascents" include one that has to do with a certain staircase in the Temple. It had fifteen steps corresponding to these fifteen psalms. Yet another theory is that these psalms evidence frequent concatenation in which a word or a phrase connects or links pairs of verses so that the psalms proceed by stages or degrees. For example, in Psalm 120 the Lord's name is in verses 1 and 2. The words "deceitful tongue" link verses 2 and 3. The English word "dwell" connects verse 5 to 6 (although two Hebrew words are here). And "peace" occurs in both verses 6 and 7. Some of the psalms are completely concatenated. See the comments on Psalm 123 for a fine example of this.

Psalm 120 is not particularly joyous. Rather, it is a kind of lament. The psalmist is complaining about those who say false and destructive things about him. Verse 1, however, does record the fact of an answered prayer, but that is the only positive verse of the seven in this brief poem. It reflects the common propensity of people to pray only in time of trouble. It is not bad to do that—unless that is the only time we do it.

Verse 2 is either a record of that prayer or a new one for a similar problem. In particular, the psalmist wishes for deliverance from those who deceive and lie. Although it might be a prayer that his own lips be pure, this is unlikely in view of verse 6.

Verse 3 is a rhetorical question answered in verse 4. The cure of hot coals for an impure tongue is similar to the episode in Isaiah 6. There a seraph cauterized the prophet's lips with a coal from off the altar.

The psalmist laments the fact that he lives among barbarians and pagans exemplified by Meshech and Kedar. The former is a place of uncertain location to the north and west. Kedar is a tribe living in the deserts to the south and east. The reference to these faraway places strengthens the assumption that this psalm is a pilgrim's song. The next two verses expand the complaint that he lives with inhospitable neighbors. "Peace" is the best translation for *shalom,* especially in contrast to the word "war'" which ends the psalm. Nevertheless, we must still bear in mind the rich, comprehensive meaning of that term. In addition to cessation of hostilities it means health, wealth, happiness, and a right relationship with God.

The question to the modern believer is this: When they speak of war, do we speak of peace?

PSALM 121

Two poetical versions of Psalm 121 appear in *The Scottish Metrical Psalter* (1650), but I prefer the paraphrase and expansion which John, Duke of Argyll, made in 1909.

Unto the hills around do I lift up
    My longing eyes:
O whence for me shall my salvation come,
    From whence arise?
From God the Lord doth come my certain aid,
    From God the Lord, who heav'n and earth hath made.

He will not suffer that thy foot be moved:
    Safe shalt thou be.
No careless slumber shall his eyelids close,
    Who keepeth thee.
Behold our God, the Lord, he slumb'reth ne'er,
    Who keepeth Israel in his holy care.

Jehovah is himself thy Keeper true,
    Thy changeless Shade;
Jehovah thy Defense on thy right hand
    Himself hath made.
And thee no sun by day shall ever smite;
    No moon shall harm thee in the silent night.

From ev'ry evil shall he keep thy soul,
    From ev'ry sin:
Jehovah shall preserve thy going out,
    Thy coming in.
Above thee watching, he whom we adore
    Shall keep thee henceforth, yea, for evermore.

Of the twenty different translations of the Old Testament in my library, only Luther's German edition and the

King James Version do not interpret the second half of verse 1 as a question. They read the word "whence" as a relative pronoun (German, *von welchen*). Kenneth Taylor departs most drastically from a straightforward translation with *The Living Bible* paraphrase: "Shall I look to the mountain gods for help?" Basically, I agree with the interpretation. The psalmist in verses 1 and 2 is asserting his confidence in the Lord who created heaven and earth, including the mountains. Help does not come from the mountains but from their Creator. Canaanites and other pagans looked to the high places for spiritual strength. Our eyes must be lifted yet higher. While the Rockies and other mountain ranges can give inspiration, and though God's hand is more obvious in spectacular landscapes, they are still only the creation and not the Creator.

The theme of God's sustenance continues through this psalm. Note the six occurrences of the word "keep" in verses 3-8 (ASV). Ours is the ever-wakeful God (v. 4). Unlike Baal whom Elijah accused of sleeping (1 Ki 18:27), the Watcher over Israel never indulges in the rest that humans require.

To people living in an arid climate, the sun is a real enemy. It burns their skin. It parches their throats. It dries up their water holes. It makes midday work unbearable. For that reason God is called a shade (v. 5) so that the sun does not strike by day (v. 6). Compare Psalm 17:8; 91:1; Isaiah 25:4; 49:10; and Jonah 4:8 for this idea.

The moon parallels the sun. In general the moon was friendlier and some ancient people deified it. But others feared it too and connected the moon with lunacy. Again Psalm 91:5-6 complements this passage. God's care is ever with us protecting us night and day, through heat and cold, from enemies human and natural.

Verses 7 and 8 expand even further the idea of God's keeping power. "Soul" in verse 7 can be understood theologically, or physically in the sense of life, or both. God preserves, spares, keeps alive, and gives longevity to those He loves. The eternal dimension comes up in verse 8. God will keep the believer now and for eternity. The "coming in" and "going out" encompass all our actions. It is an aphoristic way of describing everything we do. Deuteronomy 28:6; 31:2; Joshua 14:11; and 2 Samuel 3:25 all contain a similar statement. It is even possible to read into these words notions of the cradle and the grave. God is with us when we are born and when we die. At the death of the believer the "evermore" begins.

PSALM 122

Better than any of the other pilgrimage songs (Ps 120-34), Psalm 122 fits that category. The opening verses clearly state that those who sing this psalm are on their way to the Jerusalem Temple.

The title contains the name of David (as do Ps 124, 131, and 133 in this group). Coincidentally, David's name is in verse 5. These titles may indicate that David wrote it, that it was written for him, about him, or in his style.

As the psalms before and after it, Psalm 122 evidences staircase parallelism. "House of the LORD" and "thy gates, O Jerusalem" are synonyms. The name Jerusalem itself links verses 2 and 3. The same Hebrew word is behind the "whither" (or "to which," ASV) and the "there" in verses 4 and 5. "Thrones" appears twice in verse 5. The "peace" and "prosperity" of verse 6 echo in verse 7. "Peace" appears a third time in verse 8. The term "for the sake of" (ASV) connects the last two verses.

The psalm fits the pilgrim (or modern tourist!) who finds himself at the gate of the holy city about to ascend the final steps to his goal, the Temple of God itself. Every Christian feels a surge of excitement and hears his heart beat a little faster as he first glimpses the city of God, Jerusalem the golden. The modern city is hardly "compacted together." It suffers from urban sprawl. But the ancient city, and to a certain extent the present walled, old city of Jerusalem, fit this description. It was not and still is not a large city in size, but in importance it is the navel of the earth, the center of the world. Here Abraham built an altar; here Solomon erected the Temple; here the Son of God met and conquered death.

Most specifically verse 4 speaks of it as the focus of pilgrimages. This is the place, as Moses said many times in Deuteronomy, where God would choose to make His name dwell (see especially Deu 12, 14, 16, 17).

Exactly what "thrones of judgment" are is uncertain. Perhaps the pilgrims would bring cases for adjudication when they came to Jerusalem.

The command to pray for the peace of Jerusalem is as pertinent today as it was then, maybe more so. The Christian knows, however, that no enduring peace will come apart from the Prince of Peace who lived, died, and rose there so many years ago. Though the common Israeli greeting is *shalom* (peace), and though the meaning of the word Islam is "submission," neither the Jews nor the Muslims enjoy the other's intentions.

Jerusalem means "city of peace," and that fact may be behind the repetition of the word "shalom" in verses 6-8. The pilgrim could be representing others at the Temple, as the first half of verse 8 implies. Or it may mean that he is praying for his relatives and friends who live in Jerusalem all the time.

One of the countless benefits of Christianity is that God can be found anywhere. He is no longer localized in a building on a hill in the Middle East. Holy Land tours convey no religious merit, but prayer for Jerusalem's peace still avails.

PSALM 123

As noted previously, Psalm 123 is a fine example of concatenation. Each verse is connected with what precedes and follows it by at least one linking word. Notice the word "eyes" once in verse 1 and three times in verse 2. The prayer "have mercy" connects the end of verse 2 with verse 3, where it occurs twice. The phrase "filled with contempt"is repeated in both verses 3 and 4.

The beginning of this psalm is like Psalm 121: "I will lift up my eyes." In the latter the psalmist states, in effect, "I will not look to the hills for my strength but to the Lord." In Psalm 123 he is more straightforward.

Verse 2 has in it two illustrations: a servant looking to his master, and a maid looking to her mistress. In such a devoted and servile way the believer looks to his Lord. The idea of servitude continues into the New Testament, but the new covenant brings a new relationship between God and His child. His status is elevated, and although he is still a servant, he is also a brother of Christ and a joint heir with Him.

After the confession of devotion and allegiance in the first two verses, the actual prayer of the psalm comes in verse 3, with a complaint in verse 4. The psalmist repeats his plea, "have mercy," and the area in which he needs pity is that of persecution. Apparently he is the object of scorn and is weary of the abuse that proud and lazy men have heaped upon him.

The plaintiff began in verse 1 in the singular, "I," but from verse 2 on the petitioners are plural, "we." Such general terms as characterize these verses make it impossible to know with any assurance when the psalm was written. One theory is that it comes from the time of Nehemiah when the repairers of the Temple were harassed by outsiders.

It is preferable not to try to pinpoint the situation which prompted the psalm, but to apply the Scriptures to the innumerable trials God knew His children would face. The more imprecise the problem is, the more widely applicable is the prayer of verse 3. So whatever form the persecution of the believer takes, this psalm can serve as a model for prayer.

PSALM 124

Psalm 124 is basically a hymn praising God for deliverance. Although the enemies are human, the circumstances are illustrated by near drowning and escape from a bird trap.

Verse 1 is the introduction. Verses 2-5 describe the first harrowing experience, while verses 6-8 spell out the second. Both stanzas include benedictions or phrases of praise.

Both Psalm 124:1 and Psalm 129:1 (ASV) include the little liturgical instruction, "Let Israel now say." This phrase may reflect the way the psalm was used. Very likely the leader, a musically inclined Levite, would deacon or line out the psalm. Only the first verse shows this, but we understand the procedure would continue to the end. Lack of copies or the illiteracy of the people necessitated this.

The entire first stanza is worded in such a way that it is dependent on the opening statement, "If it had not been . . . ." Starting as it does with a kind of negative, the situation is described as if it really did happen. Of course, it did not because, as a matter of fact, God *was* on their side. The water did *not* overwhelm them.

As in the preceding psalm, the specifics of the persecution are unknown. But the effort of evil men to "swallow" the good is similar to the water swallowing a man. The Hebrews were neither swimmers nor seafarers. Few people in ancient times knew how to swim or desired to learn. In fact, the word "swim" occurs only three times in the Old Testament, in Psalm 6:6; Isaiah 25:11; and Ezekiel 47:5. Deep water was a frightening thing to most Hebrews.

In a few places in the Bible the word "soul" carries the meaning of breath, throat, or neck. Verses 4*b* and 5 may be one of those places. If one goes under water much deeper than the *neck* he cannot *breathe*. That very physical meaning of the word "soul" is quite likely meant here.

"Neck" also may be the meaning in verse 7 where "soul" is the usual translation. Some of the several varieties of bird traps undoubtedly caught the bird by the neck. On the other hand, "soul" sometimes refers simply to the person himself. The word is, after all, parallel to "we" in verse 7.

In any event, the psalmist, speaking for all who sing this hymn, escaped both drowning and capture. There is no reason to think that the enemy actually put out nets or other gadgetry to trap the righteous. Rather, the snares illustrate the sneaky, deceptive, and usually cruel methods that wicked men use.

Because of God, the trap did not work, and the intended

victims, the believers, escaped. So a benediction closes the hymn. The exalted phrase "who made heaven and earth" is contained also in Psalm 121:2. Though injustices, abuses, and narrow escapes characterize this life, God is still aware, concerned, and in complete control.

PSALM 125

Psalm 125 is a confession of trust in the Lord and a prayer for His blessing on the righteous. However, the wicked are the subject of verses 3 and 5.

Typical of the psalms of ascent, this one speaks in exalted terms of the city of Jerusalem. Zion or Mount Zion is the poetic term for the capital city. Mostly it occurs in the psalms and usually in passages which focus on its spiritual role in the nation. The original Mount Zion, or the city of David, today lies south of the Temple area outside the walled city. Its rock base is overgrown with weeds or covered by ramshackle dwellings. What today is generally called Mount Zion, the western hill immediately south of the walled city between the Tyropean and Hinnom valleys, is somewhat of a misnomer. Scholars trace the error back to Josephus, the first-century historian who, like many of us, found it hard to believe that the lesser of the two shoulders extending south was indeed the original city.

The mountain or ridge has not moved, and that is what the psalm is saying. Furthermore, the verse states that those who trust God are as unmovable as that rocky slope.

The analogy in verse 2 compares God's protection to the surrounding mountains. This is geographically accurate, since Jerusalem is located in the middle of the hill country and every horizon is punctuated by peaks. Such mountains illustrate protection. In olden times when soldiers moved only on foot there was hardly a more formidable barrier than a mountain range. Psychologically, too, mountains are beneficial. People in the mountainous areas of the United States remark that the mountains remind them constantly of their smallness and of God's greatness.

Verse 3 is somewhat difficult to understand. It is not a prayer but a statement that wickedness will not rule. Of course, it is God's protection which stems the tide of wickedness and its resultant apostasy.

In its strict division of people into two groups, Psalm 125 is reminiscent of Psalm 1. The good will inherit good things, while the crooked merit condemnation. The word for "crooked ways" in verse 5 appears only one other time in the Bible, in Judges 5:6, where it seems to mean "back roads," perhaps "detours" in the sense of "devious paths." A cognate word in Isaiah 27:1 describes a snake.

The psalm ends, as does Psalm 128, with the simple benediction, "Peace [Shalom] to Israel!" (JB).

PSALM 126

The opening verse of Psalm 126 points to its postexilic origin. The captives had dreamed so long of returning that when it happened they could hardly believe it. In Hebrew there is a play on words. The sounds of "return" and "captives" are very similar. Some translations read "fortune" for "captive" in both verses 1 and 4, but this is a matter of interpretation and not of reading a different Hebrew word (cf. RSV, NEB, Amp.).

Certain words link the psalm into an ABC, ABC pattern. Verses 1 and 4 both speak of the Lord bringing back the captives. The former is in a temporal clause; the latter is imperative. Verses 2 and 5 both have the same Hebrew word for "joy" or "singing." And verses 3 and 6 also mention "joy," though it is translated from different Hebrew words.

Note again the choice of the name Zion rather than Jerusalem. It denotes the spiritual capital of the world and the singular place of God's abode.

The first half of verse 2 is a nice parallel. The verb "filled" does double duty, carrying over from the first to the second stich. "Mouth" parallels "tongue," and "laughter" parallels "singing."

Just as in Deuteronomy 29:24-28 the nations remarked on God's punishment, so in Psalm 126:2b they noted the great things God had done for His people (cf. Eze 36:36).

The psalm turns from a hymn of thanksgiving to a prayer at verse 4, with a plea for restoration. The rivers of the south (Negev) are empty most of the time. The Arabic word for this is *wadi,* the Spanish word is *arroyo,* and the American word is *dry gulch* or *wash.* Those few times a year when the rain falls, it falls abundantly, and the gulleys become rushing torrents. That is what is behind this prayer. The people beseech God for His overflowing blessing.

Verses 5 and 6 are a pair, with the latter an expansion of the former. The King James Version is the only translation with the word "precious" in connection with seed in verse 6. Most have "seed for sowing" or the like. But three modern translations have opted for "bag" or "pouch of seed" (NEB, NASB, Anchor). It is not too critical a question. The point still remains: investment is often painful, while rewards are always welcome. Every farmer must calculate how much he can spare to sow against how much he hopes to reap. With God's blessing, a plenteous harvest is certain.

Verses 5 and 6 supply encouragement to evangelists. The weeping, the pleading, the intercessory prayer for the lost must precede the harvest of souls that every obedient Christian wishes to see. Jesus Himself compared sowing and reaping to the work of spreading the faith in His parable of the sower (Mt 13). To the sower, there is a measure of risk, even loss, in the effort to strike that propitious combination of soil, seed, climate, and care which produce enduring and abundant fruit.

PSALM 127

Of the psalms of ascent only 127 is ascribed to Solomon. The explanation for this is not easy, although some see a connection between him and the word "beloved" in verse 2. That word fills the Song of Solomon. Others see Solomon as the father of many children *par excellence*. With 700 wives and 300 concubines, his family must have been enormous!

There seem to be two parts to this little poem. The first two verses spell out the fact that without God's aid man's work is useless. The second half focuses on children as assets and the gifts of God.

The psalm opens with the well-known statements about God's necessary participation in any successful human endeavor. The Hebrew word for "house" could mean several things. The plain meaning of a dwelling is, of course, the first possibility. On a grander scale it might refer to the palace or to the Temple. In this regard the verse applies to church-building programs. "House" is also used in the sense of dynasty or family. Perhaps this is the connection between

66

the two halves of the psalm. In this sense the promise has to do with building a godly home filled with mutually loving, generous, respectful parents and children.

The second illustration, that of the watchman, also admits of several applications. We need safety not only from robbers or military foes but from the multitudes of ideas and forces that would destroy us spiritually, emotionally, and physically. These threats are both within us and without. So this is also a prayer for God's vigilance over our total being. The reference to "city" may tie in with the city "gate" in verse 5.

Verse 2 elaborates on the matter of staying awake and watching. It is not advocating a carefree abandon of all diligence, nor is it suggesting laziness. Rather, the words warn against the man who burns himself out with worries or kills himself with hard work just to have a few more shekels to spend. On the other hand, God gives the gift of sleep— sound, reviving, health-restoring, therapeutic sleep—to the ones He loves.

In the ancient world, large families, especially with many boys, were viewed as proof of God's love. Witness the dramatic events in the lives of the patriarchs in their concern over sons. Or consider the problems created when a man had only daughters such as Zelophehad (Num 27). Sons meant more hands on the farm, more children to bear the patriarch's family name, and more voices to speak in defense of the father. In fact, the last line of verse 5 has that situation in view. The many children can defend the father in the community court which meets at the city gate. A real hand-to-hand fight is not the first meaning, although that is a distinct possibility.

This heritage of the Lord is compared to a quiver full of arrows. Just as no ancient warrior would go out with just one or two arrows, so no man would be satisfied with a small number of children. Incidentally, questions of overcrowding and population explosion did not concern these people, who were far from fulfilling that cultural mandate. Furthermore, more than half the children born would not survive infancy and childhood. To have many children was a kind of insurance that a sufficient number would live long enough to perpetuate the family. The analogy of the arrows works in this dimension as well. The hunter or the soldier cannot be sure he will hit the target with each arrow, so to have several gives him a better chance. Even David had five stones in his pouch when only one was necessary to fell Goliath.

PSALM 128

Both Psalms 127 and 128 speak of the blessing of a family. Perhaps that is why they are together in the Psalter. However, Psalm 128 is broader than the preceding one and mentions both wife and children as by-products of God's blessing on those who fear Him.

This psalm divides into two halves which more or less echo each other. The first verse in the first half and the first verse in the second half (v. 4) both speak of the blessing on those who fear the Lord. In Hebrew, two different words are used. Verses 1 and 2 have the word for "happy" or "blessed," while verse 4 has the more common term for blessed. Verse 2 corresponds to verse 5. Both have the Hebrew word for "good" or "well." The last verse of each half (3 and 6, respectively) refers to children.

Also noteworthy are the three place names in verses 5 and 6. Zion is parallel to Jerusalem, while Israel is the general term for the people of God in the Old Testament, regardless of where they live.

"Blessed is every one who fears the LORD" (v. 1, NASB). This introduction to the psalm is typical of the entire collection. Psalm 1 begins in a similar way. Both Psalms (111:10) and Proverbs (1:7; 9:10) state that the fear of the LORD is the beginning of wisdom. Again remember that this fear does not exclusively mean fright but encompasses reverence, respect, and awe. The God-fearer is a person who walks in the ways of God—another idea reminiscent of Psalm 1 (vv. 1, 6).

To enjoy the fruit of one's own labor is taken for granted in our free and affluent society. But for a slave or a tenant farmer this would be an extraordinary blessing.

After independence (v. 2) comes the blessing of a fruitful wife and a large number of children. In this regard, the psalm corresponds to the preceding one. Because of the central role of wine and oil in the simple economy and diet of the Old Testament world, it is only natural that the poet compares the family to these two staples. Just as a man's wealth was counted in vineyards and olive orchards, so a man's community status was achieved by a productive wife and many offspring.

The parallel blessings in verses 5 and 6 are also noteworthy. The references to Zion and Jerusalem may indicate that this is a psalm of ascent. The blessed man of this psalm makes his annual treks to the religious capital of his nation. But more than that, he is able to go as long as he lives. Neither poor health nor poverty deprive him of this triannual spiritual experience. Verse 5b may be saying that he retires in Jerusalem.

Added to the fact that he reaches an old age is the blessing

69

of seeing his grandchildren. For people whose life spans rarely went over fifty, this was a unique blessing.

Psalm 128 ends with the same benediction that closed Psalm 125: "Peace be upon Israel (ASV). Remember the promise of Psalm 122:6? "Pray for the peace of Jerusalem: they shall prosper that love thee."

PSALM 129

Psalm 129 is one of the few imprecatory psalms (cf. Ps 69-71, and 137). The first three verses are the complaint and the last four verses are the curse.

Like Psalm 124, Psalm 129 was probably antiphonal. The instruction "Let Israel now say" (v. 1*b*, ASV) indicates that the congregation was to repeat the words of the leader. The complaints are in such general terms that it is difficult to determine to what they refer. Any date on the psalm would be a pure guess.

The persecution the psalmist and his countrymen suffered was a lifelong one. The agony they suffered felt like a plow gouging into their backs. Perhaps this refers to scourging, since a whip would leave lacerations like furrows in a field.

Verse 4 does not really belong either with the complaint section or with the curses inasmuch as the verb is not a jussive or wish-type verb. If that were true the sentence would read, "Let him cut the cords of the wicked."

Notice that the curses or imprecations follow the statement that the Lord is righteous. Neither the righteous man nor the righteous God does these things because he is unkind or hateful but because he is so concerned with righteousness, equity, and justice.

The persecutors are the haters of Zion—the very thing the righteous pilgrim loves. Zion is not merely a city, a capital, a locus for the faithful, but it is the place where God abides, His singular choice of all the cities in the world. To hate it is to hate God, and to hate God is to hate everything He is and stands for, including righteousness, mercy, integrity, and steadfast love.

The wish of verse 5 is that the persecutors be shamed and thwarted. The wish of verse 6 is that they be like the short-lived grass that grows on the flat, earthen roofs of Middle-Eastern houses after rain. The worthlessness of that grass is the subject of the next four remarks (vv. 6b-8). First, it withers before it grows up. Second, because it withers so readily, no reaper bothers to harvest it (v. 7a). Third, it does not amount to enough to bind into sheaves. And fourth, the farmers do not greet and bless each other as they work it (v. 8). Incidentally, we learn from Ruth 2:4 that the two salutations in verse 8 are the common, friendly exchanges of the workers in the field.

The point is this: No one blesses God for a worthless fistful of dried weeds. May the wicked be like that—withered, cursed, and destroyed.

PSALM 130

Psalm 130 is a prayer for forgiveness and an assertion of hope in the Lord. In several ways this psalm is like Psalm 86.

The psalm is tightly knit together with key words linking immediate and more remote verses. Note the occurrences of the divine name, Yahweh (LORD), in verses 1, 3, 5, and 7 (the form in v. 3 is shortened simply to Yah). In verses 2, 3b, and 6 the less common appellative *Adonai* (Lord) appears. The word "voice" ties together the two halves of verse 2. One of the Hebrew terms for "sin" is in verses 3 and 8. The preposition "with," in reference to God, occurs in verse 4 and twice in verse 7. "Wait" occurs twice in verse 5, while the term "soul" links verses 5 and 6. Also verses 5 and 7 share the word "hope." The same Hebrew word is the basis of "mark" in verse 3 and "watch" in verse 6. Two words, "Israel" and "redeem," are found in both verses 7 and 8.

The opening two verses are a plaintive address to a hopefully compassionate God. The depths from which the psalmist cries are figurative of the throes of despair and the slough of despondency. It is unlikely that he is literally drowning or in a deep pit.

The next two verses, 3 and 4, speak of God's forgiveness. If He did not forgive, no man could stand because all have sinned. This results in the fear of God, as verse 4b indicates. If He alone can forgive, then on Him alone can the sinner cast himself for mercy. He is the one with whom we all must deal in this matter of sin. If we pray for forgiveness He will forgive. If we persist unrepentantly He will judge.

In the third couplet, verses 5 and 6, the verb "wait" (twice in v. 5) must carry over to do triple duty in verse 6. (The KJV, ASV, and NASB all indicate this by using italics.) Other versions merely insert the word, recognizing that it is a common Hebrew literary device. If you have ever spent a sleepless night on a camping trip, you can appreciate the sentiment of verse 6. That first soft light in the eastern sky is a welcome sight indeed.

The last pair of verses is an admonition to Israel. It may be understood corporately (the entire nation) or individually (each person). The only hope is in the Lord. Two rich words describe His concern. One is mercy, loving-kindness, or steadfast love; the other is redemption. Because He *is* the former, He *does* the latter. Love prompts redemption, which in turn should move the redeemed to love Him back.

PSALM 131

Three psalms have only three verses each: Psalms 131, 133, and 134, making them second only to Psalm 117 in brevity. Psalm 131 is an assertion of personal humility (vv. 1-2) and an exhortation to hope (v. 3). Among the psalms of ascent or degrees only this one and Psalms 122, 124, and 133 are ascribed to David. Nothing within the poem excludes the possibility that Israel's most famous king wrote it.

After an initial vocative, verse 1 consists of four parallels all containing ideas of height. The psalmist denies any proud thoughts or self-aggrandizing deeds. This attitude must precede any receiving of God's blessing. He resists the proud but gives grace to the humble.

Then David compares himself to a child nursing at his mother's breast. "Weaned" (v. 2) gives the idea of a child old enough to be on solid food and independent of his mother. The root means "full" or "satisfied," so the figure here is more likely an infant just finishing a meal at his mother's breast. Compare Isaiah 11:8 where the word is used in parallel to "suckling."

The point is this: He is quiet and satisfied with what God has given him. No cause for restlessness remains in his relationship to his Maker.

Verse 3 is similar to verse 7 of the preceding psalm. Israel is enjoined to hope in the Lord from now on and until eternity.

PSALM 132

Of the fifteen songs of ascent (120-34), Psalm 132 is the most unusual. It is the longest. It is the only one to mention the Messiah. Its style is different, and it contains David's name more than any other psalm.

On the other hand, this psalm does fit the general theme of the psalms of ascent. The focus is on Jerusalem, the city of David and the Zion of God. There is some concatenation, linking of verses with key words, though it is not as tight as in the preceding psalms. Basically, the tone is positive, festive, and uplifting.

The eighteen verses of Psalm 132 fall into four more or less distinct stanzas. The first five verses focus on David's resolve to build the Temple. The next five verses sound like a hymn to accompany the arrival of the Ark of the Covenant in Jerusalem. Verses 11-13 major on God's promise to bless David's dynasty. The last five verses contain God's promise to bless Zion.

The record of David's intention to build a dwelling place for God's holy Ark appears in 2 Samuel 7 (cf. 1 Ki 8:17). The Ark had been in Kiriath-jearim at Abinadab's house (1 Sa 7:1, NASB). Verse 6 may have an alternate or abbreviated form of that name, Jaar (meaning "woods," as in some translations). From there the Ark was taken first to the house of Obed-edom and then to Jerusalem.

David did not actually build the Temple, but he is responsible for making Jerusalem the permanent resting place of the Ark. To his son Solomon goes the honor of constructing the building.

The mention of the city of Ephratah (v. 6) is somewhat enigmatic. It is an alternate name for Bethlehem (cf. Mic 5:2), the home of David. But the Ark was never in Bethlehem. It may have been in the "fields of Jaar" (RSV, NASB, *et al.*), if that is Kiriath-jearim.

The second stanza was apparently written and/or sung to commemorate the arrival of the Ark of the Covenant in Jerusalem. It is assumed that the tabernacle, the wilderness tent, still sheltered it. Verse 7 has "footstool," an interesting," epithet for that sacred chest.

The author of the psalm is unknown, but it sounds like a descendant of David, perhaps one of the more faithful kings of Judah such as Uzziah, Hezekiah, or Josiah. He calls himself "anointed" in verse 10. The Hebrew word for that is Messiah; the Greek word is Christ. However, this is not why the psalm is Messianic. It is mainly because of verse 17, which John the Baptist's father alluded to (Lu 1:69). All the kings are anointed. The term does not necessarily have prophetic significance.

More references to David's dynasty appear in verses 11 and 12. The psalmist refers to 2 Samuel 7:12-16 and Psalm 89:3-4, 35-36. It was true that as long as the kings of Judah patterned their lives after the Law of God they prospered. Over and over the books of Kings and Chronicles remark how each king did or did not do what was right in the eyes of the Lord.

Whereas verses 10-12 speak of people through whom the covenant was kept, verses 13-16 focus on the place. Zion, the spiritual Jerusalem, was the resting place for the Ark and the dwelling place of God on earth. This was so from the time David brought in the Ark around 960 B.C. until the

Babylonian captivity around 586 B.C. The records are not clear as to the disposition of the Ark after that, but we do know the Temple was functioning during the time of Christ. In A.D. 70 the Romans under Titus took away the Ark as a trophy of war. Whether it was the same one or a replica we do not know.

Notice the similarity between verses 9 and 16. This is just one example of how the psalm is integrally one. Note also the repetition of words such as dwell or dwelling, resting place, anointed, swore, and clothe.

It is at verse 17 that the psalm seems to look beyond the dynasty which ended with King Zedekiah. The sprouting horn, a symbol of strength, refers to Christ, the greater Son of David. The same figures appear in the prophecies of Isaiah (4:2); Jeremiah (23:5; 33:15); Ezekiel (29:21); and Zechariah (3:8; 6:12).

The imagery of a throne, mentioned in verse 11, is also used of Christ (Is 9:7; Lk 1:32; Ac 2:30; Rev 4:2-5). And although this word for "lamp" in verse 17 is not used, the Messiah will be a *light*. (See Is 42:6; 49:6, Lk 2:32.)

Verse 18 has the only negative note in the psalm. As the priests of Zion were clothed with salvation (v. 16), so the king's enemies will be clothed with shame. But on the Messiah's head God's crown will shine. At the first advent of Christ He wore a crown of thorns, but at the second He will be wearing one of gold (Rev 14:14).

PSALM 133

Psalm 133 is a simple and short psalm extolling the harmonious cooperation of brothers. The brothers may be only the priests, the Levites, but more likely they were the entire Israelite family, especially as they camped on the slopes surrounding Jerusalem during festivals. As more and more people poured into the holy city for each of the three annual feasts, the temporary shelters would spill down the hillsides just as the anointing oil dripped off Aaron's head onto his beard and garments.

That is a beautiful scene not unlike the thousands that Jesus addressed on the slopes near the Galilean Sea. Nor is it much different from the crowded parking lot of a Gospel-preaching church.

The unifying theme which brought these ancient believers together was God's order that all men appear in Jerusalem for the feasts of Passover, Pentecost, and Tabernacles (Deu 16:16). These pilgrimages were religious, to be sure, but they also provided a necessary change of pace. Here the men could meet their friends, share their problems, get caught up on the news, and fulfill their duty to God.

The two illustrations of fraternal concord are most interesting. The first picture is of Aaron's anointing. Exodus 30: 22-25 has the recipe for the oil and the procedure for anointing both the sacerdotal participants and the furniture and utensils. To us it may seem like a messy procedure, but we should think more in terms of furniture polish or expensive perfumed lotions. They were costly; they were fragrant; they were the finest available in the land. Aaron was the first high priest, so he represents the spiritual dimension of the pilgrimage of this psalm.

The second picture is of the dew on Mount Hermon. Hermon is the mountain to the extreme north of the promised land. At its slopes the four tributaries of the Jordan begin. Snowcapped much of the year, it symbolized abundant moisture, the gift of God to a dry land. Some wonder how any plants can survive the long, rainless summers of Palestine. But the answer is the dew. Nightly, as the temperature drops, the humidity in the air condenses to provide the needed moisture for plants. As water is a gift, so God blesses His people with unity and continuing life.

John 17 parallels Psalm 133. There Jesus prayed for the unity of believers, "that they may be one, even as we are" (v. 11, RSV). He also mentions the blessing of eternal life: "And this is life eternal, that they should know thee the only true God, and him whom thou didst send even Jesus Christ" (v. 3, ASV).

PSALM 134

The fifteen songs of ascent or psalms of degrees (KJV) end with Psalm 134. This short psalm is something of a benediction closing the collection of compositions on the same general theme. Notice that the word "bless" occurs in all three of its verses. Apparently it is some sort of a liturgical blessing similar to the high priest's benediction of Numbers 6:24-26. Just who speaks these lines is not certain. Perhaps it is the priests who bless one another. Or it may be that the worshipers and the Temple functionaries exchange these lines.

The servants of verse 1 could be either the priests or the worshipers. But those who stand nightly in the house of the Lord are more likely the professional clergy. First Chronicles 9:33 mentions certain singers who worked day and night in the Temple (cf. 1 Ch 23:30).

In verse 2 there are no prepositions in the original manuscripts between "hands" and "sanctuary," so the various translations offer different ones. The American Standard Version margin even suggests "in holiness." However, on the basis of the parallelism between house of the Lord and Zion, the majority choice of "sanctuary" is probably correct.

One might ask: How can we bless God and He also bless us? The latter is more common and easier to understand. However, "bless" is a synonym for praise. The word is related to the Hebrew word for "knee." Apparently kneeling is the posture for both blessing and being blessed. It is a two-way street. We give God blessing, and He gives it to us. We give Him what He wants, namely, praise, and He gives us what we want, namely, temporal and eternal benefactions. The questions to ask ourselves are these: Is our blessing only one way? Do we want only to get and not to give? This psalm twice urges us to bless the Lord and only once wishes God's blessing on us.

PSALM 135

A careful search will reveal that almost every one of the twenty-one verses of Psalm 135 is duplicated elsewhere in Scripture. The man who penned this psalm knew well both the Psalms and the history of Israel. Here are some of the obvious or more exact quotations.

Verse 1 is like the opening verses of Psalms 113 and 134. Verse 5*b* is similar to Psalm 95:3. Compare verses 6, 15, 16, and 18 with Psalm 115:3-6 and 8. Verses 8, 10, 11, and 12 echo in Psalm 136:10, 17-22. Verse 13 is like Psalm 102:12.

Psalm 135 clearly divides into five stanzas. The first four verses constitute the introductory volley of praise to the Lord.

The next three verses exalt the Lord as the supreme God, the One who controls the powers of nature. The longest section is verses 8-14 where the psalmist reviews God's deliverance of His people during the Exodus. Verses 15-18 approximately balance verses 5-7. They ridicule idols. Finally, the last three verses form a benediction and summons to praise. They do at the close of the psalm what verses 1-4 do at the beginning. Note that the first and last word of the psalm is "hallelujah," or in English, "Praise the LORD."

It might seem that the exhortation to praise (vv. 1-3) and later to bless (vv. 19-20) is for the professional clergy only. They are the ones who stand and serve in the courtyards of the house of God. They are of the house of Levi and Aaron. However, the command is for all the rest of Israel as well (v. 19). Ultimately, all of God's people are His servants. All believers are now Jacob and Israel (v 4). We are God's "very own" people (Tit 2:14, NIV), to give a modern flavor to the old words "peculiar people."

Verse 6 is a great one for averring the sovereignty of God. He has done whatever He pleased. This is true not only in the realm of nature, as that verse states, but also in the lives of His people. His is the only will we may not question.

From a scientific standpoint, verse 7 is interesting. Long ago when this psalm was written the author showed some understanding of the water cycle. It is obvious how water gets from the clouds to the sea, but it is not so easily observed how it gets back up in the sky again. This verse tells us.

From the subject of winds and water (v. 7) it is an easy transition to the deliverance of the Israelites out of Egypt. The very clipped résumé of the Exodus also hits the highlights of the Transjordan wars, specifically the defeat of Sihon and Og. Numbers 21:21-35 records these victories.

Three words in verses 13-14 deserve some comment. The first is "memorial" (KJV, ASV), translated "renoun" (RSV, Berkeley, NEB); "fame" (Amp); "remembrance (NASB); or "title" (NAB, Anchor). It is a synonym for "name." Note the parallel lines. Perhaps the word which is based on the basic root "to remember" is more of a commentary on the word "name" than the other way around. We are remembered by our names. It is that which represents a person in his absence. It is a handle to use in place of a more elaborate description.

The second word is "judge" in verse 14. In this context the judgment is positive, not condemnatory. Therefore, several modern translations have "vindicate." "Requite," "compensate," and "rule" are other options. Simply, the Hebrew word here is much bigger than any of our synonyms. It refers to the whole judicial process and beyond, even to governmental leadership.

The third word is "repent." Again the Hebrew word behind this is much broader and encompasses the dimensions of pity, compassion, and mercy. "Repent" implies that God has sinned. He has not. But He does show pity and exercise compassion.

The taunt song of verses 15-18 is reminiscent of what Isaiah said about idols and idolaters in Isaiah 44. These caustic jibes are in direct contrast to the words of praise the psalmist has for the creating and sustaining powers of the true God (vv. 5-7).

The concluding benediction contains three identical commands to the Israelites, the Aaronites, and the Levites. While the latter two are officially responsible to lead in worship, all Israel was to praise God.

PSALM 136

No other psalm quite compares to 136 because of its unique format. Each of the twenty-six verses ends with the refrain, "His mercy is forever." This is the clearest example of a psalm used for liturgical purposes. Most likely the song leader, a Levite or descendant of Asaph, would recite the first half of each verse and the congregation would echo the refrain. Although it may seem boring to us, we should be grateful for it and take this repetition as a reminder that all we have, are, or do depends on the constant loving-kindness of God.

The key word in the refrain is that many-faceted Hebrew term, *hesed*. No one English word covers it; therefore many different translations exist. The King James Version reads "For his mercy endureth for ever." The American Standard Version has "For his lovingkindness endureth for ever." Moffatt offered "His kindness never fails." The Improved Bible of 1913 chose, "For his mercy is forever." The Revised Standard Version renders it, "For his steadfast love endures for ever." The Berkeley Bible gives "His covenant love is everlasting." The Jerusalem Bible is, "His love is everlasting." The New English Bible employs, "His love endures for ever." The New American Bible, very close to the King James Version, opts for "For his mercy endures forever." The New American Standard Bible follows the Smith-Goodspeed 1939 translation, "For his [loving] kindness is everlasting." The Anchor Bible reads, "For his kindness is eternal." In a few of the verses *The Living Bible* expands the phrase to, "For his lovingkindness to Israel continues forever." And the best known of the several versions in the Scottish *Psalter* repeats the refrain as:

> His mercies are forever sure
> And shall for age to age endure.

All these together scarcely can bring out the richness of the words which underscore, emphasize, and enunciate the fact that God never has been and never will be anything but reliable, kind, trustworthy, faithful, and loving to His people.

Psalm 136 evidences a certain plan in its contents. The opening three verses and the closing two are somewhat of an invocation and a benediction. Note in particular the similarity between verses 2, 3, and 26. Three three-verse stanzas (4-6, 7-9, 10-12) follow, and then come three four-verse stanzas (13-16, 17-20, 21-24).

The first two stanzas after the introduction (4-9) focus on God the Creator. The next two stanzas (10-16) center on God's deliverance of His people from Egypt and, in particular, from the Red Sea episode. The last two stanzas within the body of the poem (17-24) continue the Exodus theme, with special attention to the defeat of the Amorite kings and the actual possession of the promised land. So the psalm roughly follows the progress of events from the creation in Genesis to the conquest of Canaan recorded in Joshua.

PSALM 137

This little psalm is, on the one hand, the most plaintive and, on the other hand, the most vindictive of all the psalms. It may come as a surprise to learn that the gentle sentiments of verses 1 and 2 are in the same psalm with the curses of verses 8 and 9, but they are.

The contents indicate an exilic or postexilic setting. A

captive from Jerusalem is lamenting his own misfortune and the desolation of his holy city, Jerusalem.

The first four verses bemoan the cruel taunts the captured Israelites suffered from the heartless Babylonians. Verses 5-6 are something of a vow to honor and pray for Jerusalem. The enemy Edom is the focal point of verse 7, and vicious Babylon bears the brunt of verses 8 and 9.

The rivers of Babylon are the immortal Tigris and Euphrates and the many irrigation canals interlacing the southern Mesopotamian plain. Grief prompted the exiles to abandon their songs and harps (v. 2), but the unsympathetic captors demanded in a mocking way that the Jews entertain them with the songs of Zion (v. 3). Such happiness, however, cannot be artificially generated so far from Jerusalem.

If we were to sermonize for a moment we might remember that any captivity in the Bible, be it Egyptian, Philistine, Assyrian, or Babylonian, represents domination by evil. When the believer is far from God and the company of the saints, he likewise cannot sing the Lord's song. What could be more sad than a backslidden Christian reminded of his condition by a sinner?

In the center of the psalm are two famous verses of self-malediction. The psalmist vows never to forget Jerusalem or prefer any other city over it. The penalty he wishes on himself for such failure is the loss of his right hand and the use of his tongue.

The last three verses are a curse on Edom and Babylon for the roles they played in the destruction of Jerusalem and the exile of the Jewish people. From Obadiah 11 we learn that the Edomites, the half brothers of the Israelites through Esau, stood aloof on the day of Judah's defeat. Amos 1:11 charges Edom with pursuing his brother (Israel) with a sword and never abating his anger. That Babylon, under the leadership of Nebuchadnezzar, destroyed Jerusalem needs no documentation. The divine wrath toward Babylon is a frequent theme among the prophets (Is 13, 47; Jer 25, 50, 51; Rev 18).

Many are bothered by the vengeful attitude displayed in verse 9. "How," some ask, "can any man of God make such a wish on his enemies?" Two explanations may help in understanding this. First, the "little ones" may not be the infants, as such, but all the children, that is, citizens of the wicked mother Babylon. On the other hand, none of these ancient conquerors were above such cruelty as dashing babies onto rocks (see 2 Ki 8:12). The second explanation is merely to understand that the psalmist was voicing God's holy displeasure toward this most sinful of all kingdoms. Intense love for God is coupled with intense hatred of His enemies. It is not easy to explain, as none of us loves God enough to hate that violently, but it does point out in some degree the way these ancient saints thought.

PSALM 138

Psalm 138 is basically a psalm of thanksgiving. The opening three verses are David's assertion that he will worship. Verses 4 and 5 speak of foreign kings joining in the praise. Then the last three verses are more of the psalmist's reflection on God's favor extended to him, weak and unworthy though he was. This psalm is like those very early ones in the Psalter. In fact, verse 2 is similar to Psalm 5:7 and verse 1 compares with Psalm 9:1.

A small problem arises with the meaning of "gods" in verse 1. The Jerusalem Bible and the New American Bible translate the very common Hebrew word for "god" as "angels." These "gods" are clearly not real deity. Perhaps they are pagan idols whom the psalmist wishes to chagrin. Or they may be some kind of superhuman, celestial servants such as angels. A third possibility is that they are human judges. This would agree with the "kings" of verse 4.

Note the attributes or aspects of God mentioned in verse 2: love, truth, word, and name.

It sounds as if the kings of the earth are sympathetic in verse 4. At this point the psalm might even be considered Messianic, since it speaks of the obeisance of non-Israelites. Whenever in the Old Testament we read of outsiders coming to God there is a futuristic, Church-age ring to the verses under consideration.

The closing three verses (6-8) give more of the reason for this praise. David is again, as often before, reflecting on the protection God gave him from his enemies. The oft-quoted promise of verse 8 is somewhat elliptical. Of the many ways to spell out its meaning with additional words, the New English Bible is commendable. It has "The Lord will accomplish his purpose for me." That translation brings to mind Philippians 1:6: "He who began a good work in you will carry it on to completion until the day of Christ Jesus" (NIV).

PSALM 139

No other passage of Scripture quite compares with Psalm 139 for teaching what the omnipresence and omniscience of God mean. In most beautiful terms these assuring doctrines permeate this ancient psalm of David. So rich and fascinating a work is it that Edward J. Young wrote an entire book on this psalm alone.*

The twenty-four verses are divided into four sections of six verses each. The first six speak of God's omnipresence. The next six spell out the dimensions of His all-knowing concern. Verses 13-18 focus on God's role in our lives from a time before birth. The concluding six verses are the psalmist's response of hatred toward sin and an invitation to God to examine him. Note the "search" that both opens and closes this magnificent psalm (vv. 1, 23).

God knows everything. He even knows what we think. Of course He knows what we say. These truths are repeated several times in different ways throughout the opening verses of Psalm 139. Then verse 6 is a kind of doxology.

That God knows so much can be both disconcerting and comforting. It is foolish to suppose we can think evil and He not know it. Certain sins are sins of the mind, such as lust and pride. But in God's sight they are just as sinful as those wicked acts the hands can do.

It is also reassuring to know that God reads our motives and understands our intentions even when others do not. How wonderful to know that God sees and sympathizes with our most unspeakable problems! This also means that He knows everyone else's thought life and that He will hold all men accountable, even for what they think.

Just as it is impossible to think anything without God knowing it, so it is impossible to be in any place where He is not present. The dimensions of height and depth (v. 8) and of east and west (v. 9) are all within God's omnipresent purview. The psalmist speaks from a position of fellowship

*Psalm 139, A Study in the Omniscience of God (London: Banner of Truth Trust, 1965).

87

and peace with God. That God is everywhere does not frighten him; rather, it is a comfort. Even the dimension of darkness does not hinder God's ability to see and hence protect His servant. Many a Christian soldier in a dark, distant, and dangerous place has claimed the enduring truth of verses 7-12.

Verses 13-16 expand on God's knowledge of our prenatal condition. Those who oppose abortion rightly quote these verses to show that God is intensely aware of, and carefully at work with, even the unborn. Notice the words that emphasize the mystery of a developing human life: fearful, wonderful, hidden, secret, and curiously.

This section too, like the first (v. 6), ends with a doxology (vv. 17-18). Certainly God thinks of us more often and with more intensity than we do of Him. The last phrase of verse 18 is one of several problem passages in this psalm. The gist may be, as the New English Bible has paraphrased it, "To finish the count, my years must equal thine."

The last six verses seem somewhat foreign to the rest of the psalm. Suddenly this beatific poet starts hurling caustic barbs at his enemies. Despite the traditional interpretation of this passage, maybe we should understand the wicked ones to be the carnal thoughts of the believing writer. Even if it does violence to interpret the verses that way, at least we can apply them so. We must come to hate the lusts and urgings, the promptings and pulses of the old nature that still thrive within us. Let us learn to hate those fleshly passions that take our minds off God and make us think, look, and act like unregenerate men.

This view of the maledictory section (vv. 19-22) finds support in the prayer which closes the psalm (vv. 23-24). The psalmist asks that God scrutinize his heart and mind for any of those wicked patterns and motives that he has just cursed.

In some respects these verses are like the final verses of Psalm 19. There David spelled out the good and pure thought life and prayed that such would mark him. Here he describes the vicious and godless thought process and prays that such will not depict him.

All in all this is a rich devotional psalm. The continual study of it, praying the concluding prayer, will help any believer walk "in the way everlasting."

PSALM 140

Psalm 140 is basically a prayer for protection from wicked men. A "selah" appears after each group of six stichs (vv. 3, 5, 8). We would expect others after verses 10, 11, and 13, but they are not there. Whatever the meaning of the term is, it does not always break the psalms according to sense.

Apart from the three words of petition ("deliver" and "preserve," v. 1, and "keep," v. 4), the first five verses of the psalm are David's complaint. Then verses 6 and 7 are a kind of statement of faith. Next come four verses constituting a prayer against the wicked (vv. 8-11). The last two verses correspond to verses 6 and 7 as a confession of trust. In simple outline the psalm develops like this:

> A Complaint (vv. 1-5)
> B Confession (vv. 6-7)
> A Curse (vv. 8-11)
> B Confession (vv. 12-13)

In other places the connivings of the enemy are compared to the setting of traps (cf. Ps 9:15; 31:4; 35:7; 57:6; 64:5).

One of several rare and hence uncertain words in this psalm is translated "adder" in the standard versions. Others are the words "desires" and "wicked device" (v. 8) and "overthrow" (v. 11).

After a well-worded complaint and a typical statement of trust in the first seven verses, the psalm takes a turn at verse 8. Here begins the imprecatory section where David prays down God's curses on his foes. As with other psalms (e. g., 69:22-28 and 137:7-9) which invoke God's wrath, the interpreter is hard pressed to explain and apply the Scripture. The usual answer is this: David so loved God and hated wickedness that he prayed for the demise of those who practiced it. This was, after all, more typical of the pre-Christian law of retaliation. As New Testament believers we should try in our passions to separate the act from the actor, the sin from the sinner.

If we cannot maintain composure while hating evil, or hate it apart from the one who practices it, then perhaps we had best withdraw from the fray, repeat verse 12 of this psalm, and wait for God to judge. It may seem as though we are losing the war against sin, but David reminds us that God will vindicate the righteous and exonerate the upright.

PSALM 141

For such a short psalm, number 141 has several difficulties in it. In fact, for the last seven of the ten brief verses there are variant readings in Hebrew and other language manuscripts, or suggested emendations to relieve the problems.

In general this is a prayer for deliverance from wicked men and sinful practices. Because "evening" is mentioned in verse 2, this is commonly thought of as an evening prayer. The title ascribes the psalm to David, but there are not enough internal clues to pinpoint the circumstances which prompted it.

Different editions of the English Bible and the commentaries outline the psalm in various ways. I prefer to see three parts: 1-2, 3-7, and 8-10. Note that the divine name occurs only in the first verse of each of these sections. The first part is an introduction or invocation. The second is the body of the prayer. And the third is a review of the whole.

In the introduction the psalmist reminds God of his urgency. It appears that the situation is growing desperate, and need for divine intervention is becoming more pressing. Verse 2 compares prayer to smoke rising from incense and the lifted up evening offering.

The best known verse of the psalm is the third. Fortunately, there is no question about the meaning of this simple request, "Set a watch, O Lord, before my mouth." Who of us should not pray it more often? This begins the section where the psalmist asks not to fall into sin. Not only does he pray for a bridled tongue but also for pure intentions (v. 4a). He knows that temptations will arise to share the food and ultimately the way of life of wicked men.

Verse 5 is similar to Proverbs 27:6, "Faithful are the wounds of a friend." Some of the ancient versions read the second line of verse 5 as the opposite: "But let the oil of the wicked never anoint my head" (RSV).

The diffculties continue with verses 6 and 7. Among several suggestions are "their bones" rather than "our bones" (v. 7). The two verses then describe the downfall and demise of the wicked.

The concluding three verses review the main points of the psalm. First comes an affirmation of faith in verse 8a.

Then verses 8*b* and 9 rehearse the prayer for protection from the traps of evil people. "Gins" were a type of snare (cf. Ps 140:5). The last verse echoes the imprecation section (vv. 6-7).

The lesson for the modern Christian is this: Keep a sweet spirit and a close relationship with the Lord, especially when the enemy seeks to lure you into sin. In particular, adopt the attitude of verse 3. If we are interpreting the last stichs of verses 5 and 6 correctly, they suggest the same gentle demeanor, even in the face of most distressing circumstances.

PSALM 142

Psalms 140-44 are all of the "trouble and trust" variety. Although Psalm 142 is sometimes labeled a personal lament or a prayer, it still follows basically the same pattern as the two preceding psalms and the two following ones. First comes the address or invocation, then the complaint, and finally the statement of confidence.

The title of Psalm 142 is similar to that of Psalm 57—a *maskil* of David when he was in the cave. The record of this episode is either in 1 Samuel 22:1 or 1 Samuel 24:3. The former passage speaks of David hiding in the cave of Adullum in the Philistine foothills. To him were gathered the riffraff of the countryside. The latter Samuel passage has David in another cave in the Judean desert near En-gedi. On this occasion David cut off the edge of Saul's robe. Both episodes were occasioned by Saul's pursuit of David. Therefore, the title to this psalm fits well with the contents, which evidence a man wrongfully persecuted and innocently pursued.

Verses 1 and 2 constitute the introduction. Note the four first-person verbs: "I cry," "I make supplication," and "I declare" (NASB). In these two verses God is addressed in the third person: him. In the rest of the psalm David uses the second person: you. Verses 3-7 are the actual prayer.

The assertions of trust are sprinkled through the body of the prayer. In verse 3 is the statement, "Thou knewest my path." In verse 5 are the words, "Thou art my refuge." And in verse 7 notice the expression of hope: "You will deal bountifully with me."

Not all David's complaints are about his personal enemy, Saul, although some certainly refer to him. The end of verse 3 records how his enemies set a trap. They are called "persecutors" in verse 6. The "prison" of verse 7 may be the cave where David could have been so easily trapped by Saul and his men.

The other "enemies" are of a different nature. The beginning of verse 3 seems to speak of discouragement, a formidable foe in itself. The thrust of verse 4 appears to be loneliness. And verse 6 may hint at more discouragement, or what in modern terminology is called an inadequate self-image or low ego-power.

Whatever or whoever the adversary was, David saw his only hope to be God. If the Lord did not help him avoid the snare, if God were not on his right hand, if God did not listen to his cry, if God were not stronger than his foes, if God would not send righteous friends to surround him, he would certainly perish at the hands of those who hated him.

Our problems may not appear as dramatic, but they are just as real, just as debilitating, just as overwhelming, just as frightening. Whether our enemy is a person or a set of circumstances, our only hope is in the Lord. He still desires to shower His children with good things.

93

PSALM 143

This psalm continues David's prayer for deliverance from his enemies. The first two verses are introductory. Again there follows a section of complaint (vv. 3-6). And again the psalm ends with a series of petitions for personal safety and for the enemy's demise (vv. 7-12).

Paul the apostle, in both Romans 3:20 and Galatians 2:16, echoes the truth of verse 2b that no one is righteous in God's sight. We often think of the Old Testament saints having an inadequate theology and perhaps even a trust in works. But this verse disabuses us of that erroneous idea. At least the enlightened saints of the older dispensation saw that salvation is totally of grace and without dependence on works. No man can measure himself by God's righteous standard and be judged adequate. So David prays knowing full well that he deserves condemnation. He has no claim on God except a plea for mercy.

Having opened the prayer and confessed in a measure his own unworthiness, David proceeds in verse 3 to outline his troubles. All of the terms are quite general, so it is impossible to determine the exact nature of the enemy's persecution. However, the "darkness" of verse 3 may allude to the cave experience mentioned in the previous psalm. In many instances caves served as graves.

Verses 5 and 6 are not exactly complaints but protestations of sincerity. David is reminding God of how faithfully he has honored and served Him. There is a certain tone of despair to verse 6, as if he were complaining of God's apathy and lack of response.

The verbs of petition begin again at verse 7. These are the first imperatives since verse 2. Count how many there are: *hurry, hide not, let hear, inform, deliver, teach, lead,* and *revive.* Verse 12 has two prayers against the adversary: "cut off" and "destroy."

Notice that after each imperative follows an affirmation of faith or a statement of his personal distress. So in verse 7 we read that his spirit is failing, in verse 8 that he trusts in God, in verse 9 that he flees to God for safety, and so on. This represents a nice balance in prayer. Often we hear only the thoughtless "bless us" or "bless them." Here is a more mature mixture of supplication, praise, thanksgiving, and confession.

Again the slightly embarrassing imprecations conclude the psalm. How can a godly man pray for God to punish the enemy? This seems especially incongruous in verse 12 where the text states, "In thy *lovingkindness* cut off mine enemies" (ASV). Once more it is that theologically rich term, *hesed.* One of the several facets of that Hebrew word is faithfulness to covenant promise. David is calling on God to keep His promise, perhaps with Deuteronomy 28:7 in mind:

> The LORD shall cause thine enemies that rise up against thee to be smitten before thy face. They shall come out against thee one way and flee before thee seven ways.

The lever the psalmist is using is God's honor. If the LORD promised then, now is the time to fulfill. Several modern translations (such as The Jerusalem Bible and The New English Bible) focus on God's love. But the translation "love" is not quite on target. The emphasis here is on God's dependability. David is concerned both with his own safety and with God's reputation for keeping the terms of the covenant which He Himself drew up.

PSALM 144

The final volley of praise which concludes the Psalter begins with Psalm 144. While 144-46 are more or less personal (with the use of *I, my, me*), Psalms 147-50 are community hymns. First the praise is personal, then the nation is admonished to exalt God, and finally everything with breath is urged to praise the LORD (150:6).

This psalm is difficult to outline, and agreement between commentators or editions of the Bible is hard to find. Many parts of the psalm are found elsewhere. Verse 1*a* is like 18:34 and 46; verse 2 compares with 18:2 and 47; verse 3 reads the same as 8:4; verse 4 comes from 39:6 and 102:11; verse 5 echoes 18:9 and 104:32; verse 6 is similar to 18:14; verse 7 harks back to 18:16; verse 9 is close to 33:2-3; verse 10 agrees with 18:50; and verse 15*b* is the same as 33:12*a* It is interesting too that Psalm 18, from which so many of the ideas in this psalm come, is also found in 2 Samuel 22.

The opening two verses have a military tone. Perhaps David is reflecting on a recent victory and is giving God the credit. God is his fortress, his Saviour, his shield, and his refuge.

A somewhat disjointed meditation on the frailty of man follows (vv. 3-4). Verse 3 is quoted in Hebrews 2:6, but the Hebrews quotation continues with the verses that follow in Psalm 8:4.

In contrast to the finitude and insignificance of men, the psalmist records a series of commands to God. Most of these contrast the power of God to the weakness of man. First, even to reach man, there is the prayer: "Bow thy heavens, O LORD, and come down" (v. 5). Then follow several ideas relative to the demonstration of divine power in nature. Toward the end of that section (vv. 5-8) is a little gibe at the enemy.

At verse 9 the Psalm takes another tack. Once more there is a series of accolades. God is praised as the One who saves and rescues. Since He is the only One who can do that, verse 11 is a prayer that He will. This stanza, like the preceding one, ends with a remark about how deceitful are the ways of the foe (cf. vv. 8, 11).

The mention of David in verse 10 does not prove that he could not have written the psalm. The Pentateuch, written by Moses constantly refers to its author in the third person.

The last section of the psalm (vv. 12-15) is the most original, that is, these verses contain few allusions to other psalms. Also, the character is different because of the grammar. Technically, there are no finite verbs—just a list of ideal and blessed conditions. A relative pronoun begins verse 12. Therefore, some translations give the list in a straightforward, indicative style. Some use jussives (i.e., wish-type verbs, "may our sons"). Still others relate everything to the last verse. I prefer this last option as a way to understand the passage, although not necessarily as a translation. Here is how it would read:

> Happy are the people whose young sons are like grown
> plants,
> whose daughters are like pillars designed for a temple.

This certainly is a beatific picture: strong sons, beautiful daughters, full barns, productive cattle, and abundant fields. At the end of verse 14 are certain things blessed for their absence: no violence, no call to arms, no screaming in the streets.

The formula a nation must follow to achieve such bliss is simple. All it must do is make Yahweh, the God of the Bible, its God. It may seem overly simplistic, but such a little sentence implies a lot. It involves following His commands, honoring His Word, receiving His Son, listening to His voice, and waiting for His justice.

PSALM 145

Psalm 145 is among the alphabetic acrostics. Each verse begins with the successive letter of the Hebrew alphabet. However, the letter *nun* is missing between verses 13 and 14 so the psalm has only twenty-one verses while there are twenty-two letters in the alphabet. (Cf. Ps 25; 34; 111; 112; 119; and each chapter in Lamentations.)

This psalm is the last one in the collection with a title. And that title is merely "Praise. Of David." The beginning of a subscription is found in a Dead Sea Scroll, but all is lost except the words, "This is for a memorial."

The hallelujah psalms begin with 146 and continue to the end, but this praise psalm is not included with the praise group in the synagogue liturgy.

No outline fits very neatly onto these verses. The reason may be that the writer was too concerned with his alphabetic device to think of subpoints and the like. The main theme which does pervade the work is the goodness and greatness of God. For the most part it is personal, with the pronoun *I* quite prominent, especially in the first six verses.

As is typical of Hebrew poetry, God is spoken of in both the second and third persons. Note the use of *you* in verse 1 and elsewhere but *his* in verse 12.

The psalm is so rich in words of praise it is hard to know what to underscore. The *Scottish Metrical Psalter* of 1650 has no less than six entries based on Psalm 145. A modern popular hymnal lists four anthems based on verses from this psalm. Here are the five short stanzas of a version written in 1824 by Richard Mant.

> God, my King, thy might confessing,
>   Ever will I bless thy Name;
> Day by day thy throne addressing,
>   Still will I thy praise proclaim
>
> Honor great our God befitteth;
>   Who his majesty can reach?
> Age to age his works transmitteth,
>   Age to age his pow'r shall teach.
>
> They shall talk of all thy glory,
>   On thy might and greatness dwell,
> Speak of thy dread acts the story,
>   And thy deeds of wonder tell.
>
> Nor shall fail from mem'ry's treasure
>   Works by love and mercy wrought;
> Works of love surpassing measure,
>   Works of mercy passing thought.
>
> Full of kindness and compassion,
>   Slow to anger, vast in love,
> God is good to all creation;
>   All his works his goodness prove.
>
> All thy works, O Lord, shall bless thee;
>   Thee shall all thy saints adore;
> King supreme shall they confess thee,
>   And proclaim thy sovereign pow'r.

Although the whole psalm can be a great benefit to worship, the following ideas should be emphasized: verse 2 suggests daily worship—not just weekly, or worse yet, twice a year. If you think you have said everything you can in praise or have exhausted your thoughts on God, remember verse 3: "His greatness is unsearchable."

Verse 4 speaks of the oral tradition. God's renown was passed from father to son through many generations. The proliferation of books and widespread literature about Him is a rather modern development.

Verses 8 and 9 focus on God's attributes and, in particular, on His goodness to the entire creation.

The word "saints" in verse 10 is built on the term *hesed* discussed elsewhere. It implies people who are faithful in covenant-keeping and steadfast in their love to God.

Verse 12 speaks to the matter of outreach. These saints declare to others what God has done. This, after all, is what evangelism is: simply telling the Good News of what God has done.

Verses 14-16 express some of the tenderness of God. Note especially verse 15, which speaks of all the world waiting for the light of day, the warmth of the sun, the freshness of spring, and the harvest of fall. All these benefits come from God's opened hand.

Verse 18 hints at a later dispensation when it would no longer be necessary to find God in Jerusalem or at any earthly sanctuary. He would be available to anyone, anywhere, anytime. He would be near to that person who would truly call on Him.

PSALM 146

Psalms 146-50 all begin and end with the Hebrew word "hallelujah" which means "praise the LORD." For that reason the Hebrews grouped these psalms together in their liturgy and called them a third Hallel. Other Hallels were Psalms 113-18 and Psalm 136.

This psalm falls easily into an outline. The first two verses form the introduction. Verses 3 and 4 focus on the basic untrustworthiness and brevity of men. The body of the poem describes God's works and wonders (vv. 5-9). The last verse is the conclusion.

Needless to say, this psalm and those following belong to the category of praise psalms. The opening words strike that note. Observe the synonymous parallelism, which is typical of the poetry of the Hebrew Bible. In verse 2 "I will praise" is parallel to "I will sing." The two divine names "Lord" (Yahweh) and "God" ('Elohim) balance each other. And the pair of temporal clauses complement each other: "while I live" and "while I have being" (RSV).

On the negative side, the psalmist urges us not to trust in men, either the noble ones or the base ones. The latter is the meaning of "son of man" in this context. The reason for such advice is that human beings simply do not last long. Soon each man's breath will be gone and his body will turn into dust. Verse 4 contains a rare word; in fact, it occurs only here in the Hebrew Old Testament. The King James Version and American Standard Version translate it "thoughts" while the Revised Standard Version, Berkeley, and the New American Bible offer "plans."

Verse 5 introduces the main part of the poem, which is a series of participles describing God's activity. Rather than trust in men, the happy or blessed hopes in the Lord, the God of Jacob.

Eleven active verbs follow to delineate God's manifold work. The list begins with God as the Creator and Sustainer and ends with Him as the Rewarder and Judge. The middle

101

part of the list (vv. 7-9) mostly emphasizes the merciful and generous features of God's concern for His creation.

The divine doings seem to come in pairs, whereas the verse numbers put them in triplets. So verses 6b and 7a go together—He keeps truth and executes justice. Then the last two stichs of verse 7 are a couplet—He gives food and frees prisoners. The first two-thirds of verse 8 describes His concern for the blind and the lame. Verses 8c and 9a likewise are a couplet—He loves the righteous and preserves the stranger.

Some scholars think 8c should be linked to 9c so that God's benefits to strangers, orphans, and widows may be one group, while the righteous and the wicked are put into an antithetical pair. The Jerusalem Bible has so arranged the verses.

A number of these actions are the same as the ones Christ did (cf. Is 61:1; Lk 4:18; Mt 11:5). Two, in particular, illustrate salvation. The Gospel frees from the prison house of sin (v. 7c), and the opening of blind eyes describes an understanding of the Christian message.

Even in judgment God is worthy of praise. He will reward the wicked man for his deeds. This last line of verse 9 recalls the last verse of Psalm 1 (RSV): "The LORD knows the way of the righteous, but the way of the wicked will perish." Another similarity to Psalm 1 comes in the choice of the word "happy" or "blessed" (cf. Ps 146:5 and 1:1).

A kind of benediction closes this psalm. Zion, the holy city of God, representing all true worshipers, is assured that her God will reign forever. He is not like transient men, but He is God for all generations. Praise the LORD!

PSALM 147

In the Greek and Latin Bibles, Psalm 147 comprises two psalms. The numbering which got off when they put Psalms 9 and 10 together is finally straightened out, so these versions also end with 150 psalms. The break in the psalm comes between verses 11 and 12.

This psalm of twenty verses does, however, show unity. It begins and ends with the word "hallelujah." It speaks of Jerusalem in both parts (vv. 2, 12). The major theme throughout is the concern of God for His entire creation—animals and man, the heavens and the earth.

Verses 1, 7, 12, and 20 have the only imperatives. These break the psalm into three stanzas, before verse 7 and before verse 12. The second break corresponds to the division of the psalm into two parts in the Greek and Latin versions. It is also interesting to note that God's proper name, Yahweh (LORD), occurs in the opening and closing verses of each of these three stanzas. Notice it in verses 1, 2, and 6; 7 and 11; 12 and 20. Actually, in verses 1 and 20 the name is shortened to "Yah," the last syllable of the word "hallelujah."

The opening verse is an introduction to the entire poem. It can be understood either that "it [praise] is good" or "He [God] is good." In the second half of the verse it is better to understand the subject as praise because the adjective "comely" and "pleasant" do not fit well with God as the subject.

Because of the reference to exiles in verse 2, the psalm may have been composed after the return from Babylon. Verses 2, 3, 4, and 6 state a number of acts God does for the world as a whole and for people in particular. In contrast to the heathen deities who were assigned various ministries, the true God is concerned both with the stars of heaven and with the broken hearts of suffering humanity. Though He numbers and names the stars, He also upholds the meek of the earth. It is no wonder the psalmist interrupted his train of thought at verse 5 to interject a doxology. He stops to magnify God's power, might, and infinite understanding.

Verse 7 is another summons to praise and an introduction to a stanza. This time, rather than starting at the bottom with the outcasts and the crushed and ending with celestial bodies, he begins with the heavens (v. 8) and concludes with the humble worshipers (v. 11).

These verses provide an interesting insight into the ancient understanding of the life cycle. First there are the clouds (v. 8a), then the rains on the earth (v. 8b), and finally the grass on the mountains (v. 8c). This, in turn, is food for the animals (v. 9).

The third stanza begins with particular focus on the city of God, Jerusalem (vv. 12-13). From there the scope of God's blessing involves the entire promised land (v. 14), and ultimately the whole earth (vv. 15-18). Zion is blessed with people once more after a seventy-year exile. Once more Canaan is filled with political peace and economic prosperity. All because, in His sovereignty, God has chosen to do it so.

Verses 15-19 provide a mixture of ideas. First there is God's irresistible and irrevocable word (vv. 15, 18, 19). Also, there is the weather, likewise sent at His bidding: snow and frost (v. 16), ice and cold (v. 17), wind and water (v. 18). At verse 18 these two streams of thought cross. There the word melts the snow and ice.

The analogy between these two leading ideas is simple. God's word is a gift like the moisture that comes with snow, rain, and frost. Although the cold is welcome because it brings moisture, it may also bring discomfort (v. 17). Anyone who has spent a winter in Jerusalem in a building that is not centrally heated can appreciate this. But the word of God brings both refreshment and discomfort. That is why this analogy is particularly interesting and beautiful. It is uncomfortable to read about our sin in the Bible, but it is pleasant to learn of the remedy in Christ.

Ancient Israel alone was the recipient of the blessing of the word of God. No other nations knew of it. Today, it is with the Church God has deposited His Word. But rather than selfishly hoard it, our duty is cheerfully to spread it. Who would deny water to a thirsty man? Who would withhold the Gospel from a dying soul?

PSALM 148

All agree that Psalm 148 has three parts. Verses 1-6 enjoin the heavens and the heavenly bodies to praise the Lord. The middle section, verses 7-10, exhorts the creation on earth to praise the Lord. The concluding four verses address the people and urge them to praise the Lord.

A "hallelujah" opens and closes the psalm. The word "praise" occurs thirteen times in these fourteen brief verses. Most of these are in the first four verses, where each stich has the word "praise."

A few of the terms merit some comment. The "hosts" in verse 2 is parallel to "angels" and, in this instance, refers to the army of assistants whom God uses for the operation of the universe. Elsewhere it often seems to mean stars, and that is still a possibility here. Verse 4 has the superlative "heaven of heavens," which is sometimes translated "highest heavens" (RSV). A text for the fiat or command creation is verse 5b: "He commanded, and they were established."

From the heights above, the psalmist moves to the depths below in verse 7. First he mentions the sea and its inhabitants. Then in verse 8 he speaks of the elements that make up the weather. In verse 9 he describes the physical features of the land and what grows on it, and finally he considers the animals. The Jerusalem Bible uses a very succinct method to render these verses:

> Mountains and hills,
> orchards and forests,
> wild animals and farm animals,
> snakes and birds . . . .

In the final part of the psalm the focus is on human beings in all categories. The first category is the leadership: kings, princes, and judges. Verse 12 includes both sexes and the extremes of age.

Verse 13 is a wrap-up. All the above creation—animate and inanimate, animal and human—is to praise the Lord. As the psalm begins with heaven, so in verse 13b we once again lift our eyes upward.

Whereas verses 5 and 6 reflect on God's concern for the heavenly hosts, verse 14 recollects the Lord's goodness to His people. The word "horn" symbolizes strength because the strongest animals wore horns. A large horn belongs to a particularly fine specimen of a bull or ox. So, figuratively speaking, God's people now share that kind of strength.

PSALM 149

Psalm 149 has a militaristic overtone to its basic theme of praise. This appears most notably from verse 6 onward. In fact, the psalm has a division at that point. Verses 1-5 are a series of oblique commands to praise. But verses 6-9 speak of God's people executing His judgment on the unbelieving.

As with its neighboring psalms, this one opens and closes with a "hallelujah" or, in English, "Praise the LORD!" The command to sing a "new song" is found often throughout the Psalter. (Note Ps 33:3; 40:3; 96:1; 98:1; 144:9).

The word "saints" in verses 1 and 5 is interesting. It is built from the term *hesed,* meaning faithful, loving, dependable, merciful, and a lot more. Usually the Bible speaks of God's *hesed* as an attribute that is communicable; it can be shared by us. We cannot be omnipresent but we can be kind. We cannot be omnipotent but we can be trustworthy. We cannot be omniscient but we can be loving.

From verse 2 on the verbs are jussives or wish forms commonly translated "let." Another way to translate the idiom is with "should"—"Israel should rejoice in his Creator," and so forth.

Among the media used to praise the Lord, according to verse 3, is the dance. Needless to say, this is not a reference to ballroom dancing or, for that matter, to any dance which involves couples only. The Amplified Bible modifies the term "dance" with the bracketed words "single or group." This is correct.

The secondary theme of the psalm, victory in battle, may be hinted at in verse 4b. The term "salvation" in the Old Testament usually means deliverance from some temporal danger, such as a political foe, a dread disease, or the threat of death. Therefore, verse 4 may be speaking of God's gift of victory to His people.

The reference in verse 5 to singing for joy in bed may seem strange. At least two explanations are possible. Now that the victory has been won, God's people can relax and rejoice. Or it may mean that even at night songs of exaltation are in order. Praise is not just a daytime activity, certainly not a once-a-week exercise.

The presence of "sword in hand" in verse 6 interrupts the otherwise lofty tone of this psalm. The psalm may have been used as a battle cry, or it may refer to the end of the age when God's people will assist Him in the righteous rule of the earth. In a sense, the conquest of Canaan was a punishment on the Amorites (Gen 15:16). And the Israelites were the agents of God to punish them.

Verse 9 has a little word that may confirm this interpretation. The judgment or verdict was already *written,* that is, the heathen deserve the sword of vengeance. God chose to give His people the honor of executing His wrath. It is difficult to reconcile this with the New Testament teaching on love of enemies, but this will have to be understood in the same way as the imprecatory psalms. Even in the exaction of punishment and the execution of justice the Lord is worthy of praise.

PSALM 150

Each of the five books within the Psalter ends with a dox-ology. (Note Ps 41:13; 72:18-19; 89:52; 106:48). Psalm 150 in its entirety is a doxology. It concludes not only the fifth book of the Psalter, but the entire collection of psalms.

No other psalm is quite like it for its repetition of the word "praise." None compares to the universality of the summons to honor God. The word "praise," in one form or another, occurs thirteen times within the brief scope of these six verses. Included in this count are the "hallelujahs" which open and close the poem.

In verse 1 the exhortation is to praise God on earth and in heaven. That is probably the meaning of the terms "sanc-tuary" and "firmament of his power." There should be an echo in heaven of the volley of praise sung in the Temple. And the Temple, in turn, should reverberate with the sound of the heavenly choir.

Verse 2 states the reasons for praise: God is great and has done great things.

Verse 3 begins the list of instruments of praise. The first is the *shofar* or ram's horn, commonly translated "trumpet." It is not like the modern cornet with valves, but is capable of changes in notes only as the player adjusts his lips to the force of his breath.

At the end of verse 3 come the *nevel* and the *kinnor,* both stringed instruments. They are portable harps which vary in size and number of strings, the *nevel* being the larger and more complicated of the two.

The *tof* (timbrel) of verse 4 is somewhat similar to a tam-bourine. It belongs in the percussion family. The dance, or in Hebrew the *mahol,* though not an instrument, is nevertheless a way to express praise. This may have been highly organized choreography performed by the priests and Levites, or it may have been the jubilation of the people as a whole.

Two instruments are mentioned in the last half of verse 4. The "stringed instruments" (Heb., *minnim*) are spoken of only here and in Psalm 45:8. The "pipe" ("organs," KJV) is probably a very simple flute or whistle not unlike those that children play.

Verse 5 refers to two kinds of cymbals. The Hebrew word *tsiltsel* sounds like the noise these devices make. The difference between the two types is uncertain. One may be soft and the other loud, or one mellow and the other harsh. Or they may be the synonyms "clashing" and "clanging," as The Jerusalem Bible suggests.

The grand finale comes in verse 6 where every living thing is urged to praise the Lord. The command is that every breath be used either to blow a horn or sing an anthem to the everlasting praise of God.

Ultimately this is the whole message of the book of Psalms: Praise the Lord! The chief end of man, according to one of the ancient creeds, is to glorify God and enjoy Him forever. And the aim of this brief commentary on the hymnbook of ancient Israel is the same. May it prompt the reader likewise to praise the Lord.

BIBLIOGRAPHY

TRANSLATIONS

American Standard Version. 1901.
Amplified Bible. 1954-65.
Anchor Bible. Psalms I, 1965; Psalms II, 1968; Psalms III, 1970.
Holy Bible: A New Translation, by James Moffatt. 1922.
Jerusalem Bible. 1966
King James Version (Authorized Version). 1611.
Modern Language Bible: New Berkeley Version in Modern English. 1959, 1969.
New American Bible. 1970.
New American Standard Bible. 1960-73.
New English Bible. 1961, 1970.
Psalms, Singing Version. 1966.
Revised Standard Version. 1946, 1952.
Scottish Metrical Psalter. 1650.
The Living Bible. 1962-71.

INTRODUCTIONS

Archer, Gleason. *A Survey of Old Testament Introduction.* Chicago: Moody, 1974.
Harrison, Roland K. *Introduction to the Old Testament.* Grand Rapids: Eerdmans, 1969.

COMMENTARIES

Calvin, John. *Calvin's Old Testament Commentaries: Psalms.* 5 vols. 1845. Reprint. Grand Rapids: Eerdmans, n.d.

Henry, Matthew. *Commentary on the Whole Bible,* vol. 3, *Job to Song of Solomon.* 1712. Reprint. Old Tappan, N.J.: Revell, n.d.

Keil, Carl F., and Delitzsch, Franz. *Commentaries on the Old Testament,* vols. 11-13, Psalms. 1867. Reprint. Grand Rapids: Eerdmans, n.d.

Leupold, H. C. *Exposition of the Psalms.* Grand Rapids: Baker, 1970.

Spurgeon, Charles H. *The Treasury of David.* Grand Rapids: Zondervan, 1970.

Yates, Kyle M. "Psalms." In *The Wycliffe Bible Commentary,* ed. Charles F. Pfeiffer and Everett F. Harrison. Chicago: Moody, 1962.

OTHER

Lewis, C. S. *Reflections on the Psalms.* New York: Harcourt Brace, 1964.